Case Studies in Strategic Planning

BOOKS BY HAKAN BÜTÜNER
FROM AUERBACH PUBLICATIONS

Planning by Design (PxD)-based Systematic Methodologies (2017)
ISBN 978-1-4987-6132-1

**Systemic Improvement Planning for Results-Based Positive
Operational Changes (2016)**
ISBN 978-1-4987-2630-6

Case Studies in Strategic Planning (2016)
ISBN 978-1-4987-5122-3

**Systematic Strategic Planning: A Comprehensive Framework for
Implementation, Control, and Evaluation (2015)**
ISBN 978-1-4987-2481-4

AUERBACH PUBLICATIONS
www.auerbach-publications.com

Case Studies in Strategic Planning

HAKAN BÜTÜNER

CRC Press
Taylor & Francis Group
Boca Raton London New York

CRC Press is an imprint of the
Taylor & Francis Group, an **informa** business
AN AUERBACH BOOK

CRC Press
Taylor & Francis Group
6000 Broken Sound Parkway NW, Suite 300
Boca Raton, FL 33487-2742

First issued in paperback 2020

© 2016 by Taylor & Francis Group, LLC
CRC Press is an imprint of Taylor & Francis Group, an Informa business

No claim to original U.S. Government works

ISBN-13: 978-1-4987-5122-3 (hbk)
ISBN-13: 978-0-367-65863-2 (pbk)

Library of Congress Cataloging-in-Publication Data

Names: Butuner, Hakan, author.
Title: Case studies in strategic planning / Hakan Butuner.
Description: Boca Raton : CRC Press, 2016. | Includes bibliographical references and index.
Identifiers: LCCN 2015034512 | ISBN 9781498751223
Subjects: LCSH: Strategic planning--Case studies.
Classification: LCC HD30.28 .B878 2016 | DDC 658.4/012--dc23
LC record available at http://lccn.loc.gov/2015034512

Visit the Taylor & Francis Web site at
http://www.taylorandfrancis.com

and the CRC Press Web site at
http://www.crcpress.com

To my great friend and wonderful human, Yıldırım Omurtag

Contents

Preface

I felt the need to show how systematic strategic planning can be used in real-life scenarios even by unskilled professionals. Accordingly, I wrote this book with the aim to let this systematic methodology and its analysis tools, based on fundamentals, be easily understood and universally applied to any type of business.

Rather than explaining the methodology and its tools (which has already been done in my previous book titled *Systematic Strategic Planning*), the intention of this book is to show how to use this methodology in developing strategic plans. But, most importantly, you are taught how to identify in what circumstances you might use specific tools and also how to target them directly at achieving effective results.

This book is organized into parts as detailed in the following. The methods and techniques, case studies, and working forms presented will guide you in preparing a strategic plan for your existing or future business:

- Part I provides the overall framework and describes the systematic pattern of strategic planning.
- Part II demonstrates case studies that were prepared by my dear students. Most of the case studies are entrepreneurial

and are of new businesses. Though the cases do not use all the sections/steps and/or techniques of systematic strategic planning, they still reflect the basics of a typical strategic plan.

This book is written mainly for two groups:

- The first group includes professional strategic planners and students who are interested in strategic planning. This group may be skilled at making strategic plans but do not fully understand that a strategic plan for any business would involve variables specific to a particular business process. Their conventional approaches must be replaced by broader analyses and individual and factual analyses of specifics by group opinions and evaluation of convenience or preference.
- The second group are professionals—people not skilled in the techniques of strategic planning. This group includes such people as owner-managers of small businesses, managers who are generally familiar with strategic planning, and department heads who have jobs that they plan to do themselves.

The content of this book has been prepared using the results obtained from applying the issue at hand to different application environments and their cause-and-effect relations. This book is a supporting material for my previous book *Systematic Strategic Planning*. It has been designed to be specific, simple to understand, and easy to use.

I owe a great debt of gratitude to all the students who contributed their case studies to the development of this book.

Most of all, I am very thankful to Richard Muther for coming up with the systematic methodology for strategic planning and for his incredible innovation for planners, which is called *Planning by Design*.

Author

 **Dr. Hakan Bütüner** is a graduate of TED Ankara College, Ankara, Turkey. He earned his BSc in industrial engineering from Middle East Technical University, MBA from Bilkent University, Ankara, Turkey, and PhD in engineering management from the University of Missouri-Rolla, Rolla, Missouri.

Dr. Bütüner has been active in both academic and professional fields for several years as planning and programming manager and as a project manager overseas. He launched and served as the chairman of a new venture that aimed at bringing various prominent international franchising concepts to Turkey.

Later, he worked as a strategic planning and business development director of Bayındır Holding, as a SPEED (operations and profit improvement program) country manager of Siemens Business Services, and as a general coordinator of Bell Holding. During the same period, he was also lecturing in various business schools and industrial engineering departments of Bilkent, Bhosporus, Bahcesehir, and Yeditepe Universities.

Dr. Bütüner is currently an affiliate of several U.S. companies involved in industrial management, engineering consulting, training, and software solutions. He is also the founder-president of the Institute of Industrial Engineers—Turkish professional chapter.

During his career, Dr. Bütüner has participated in several projects both in Turkey and abroad. He is a board member of the Institute of High Performance Planners in the United States. His other books are *Systematic Strategic Planning: A Comprehensive Framework of Implementation, Control and Evaluation; Systematic Management: Why? How?; Competitive Advantages of Object-Oriented Business System; Systematic Improvement Planning for Results-Based Positive Operational Changes;* and *Customer Initiated Business System.* He has been honored by the decision sciences society Alpha Iota Delta.

PART I

Systematic Strategic Planning (SSP)

Before beginning with strategic planning, businesses must have articulated their *missions and visions*, and identified their basic *policies*.

A strategic plan outlines the path between the current status of business and the desired status to achieve. It helps the business to establish its objectives, goals, as well as the decisions to achieve these objectives and goals. It involves a long-term and prospective perspective.

A strategic plan provides guidance for the preparation of functional plans and business budget in such a manner that they reflect the objectives, goals, and grand strategies of the strategic plan during the implementation phase, as well as for basing resource allocation on priorities. Figure P.1 shows the before and after links of strategic planning.

Functional plans help in implementation of strategic plans by organizing and activating specific subunits of the business (marketing, finance, production, etc.) to pursue the business strategy in daily activities. The greatest responsibilities are in the implementation or execution of a strategic plan. Functional plans are more specific than a business strategy to guide functional actions taken in key parts of the company to implement business strategy. Figure P.2 shows the relationship between functional and strategic plans.

Systematic strategic planning (SSP) is the pattern of procedures by which an organization defines its current status, opportunities,

Figure P.1   Strategic planning—before and after.

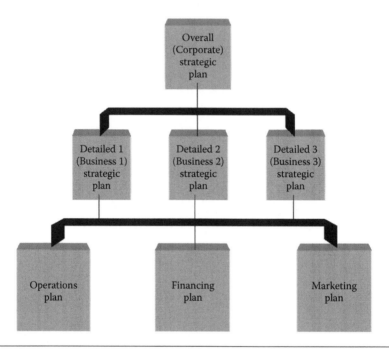

Figure P.2   Relationship between functional and strategic plans. (Reprinted from Harrison, J.S. and St. John, C,H., *Foundations in Strategic Management*, South-Western Publications, Evansville, IN, 2001.)

long-term goals, and the strategies for which to achieve them. SSP is based on the principles of *PxD* (*Planning by Design*), which is generated by Muther (2011).

SSP consists of a framework of phases through which each project passes, a pattern of sections for straightforward planning, and the fundamentals involved in any strategic planning project. Figure P.3 illustrates SSP full version.

The techniques to be used for strategic planning should not be perceived as a procedure of systematic, and the techniques used should be continuously repeatable and modifiable depending on the characteristics of individual cases.

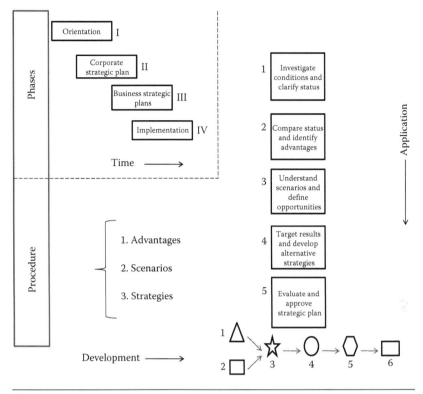

Figure P.3   SSP—reference table.

Certain working forms (in the forms of key documents and output) are used in applying the techniques in each section or steps of the SSP pattern.

In Phases II and III, the planning specialist follows a method of procedures to achieve alternative strategic plans.

In holdings/large businesses, the planning specialist uses Phase II in full SSP version to develop the overall strategic plan. The planning specialist may repeat Phase III of the full version to develop detailed strategic plans of each business/division of the holding/large business or use shortened SSP version instead if the business is small.

1

SYSTEMATIC PATTERN OF STRATEGIC PLANNING

Phases II and III are comprised of the five sections of systemic strategic planning (SSP) illustrated in Figure 1.1. For the sake of this book, only the first four sections are applied for the example cases; the fifth section is not explained as it has already been discussed in detail in my previous book titled *Systematic Strategic Planning*.

1.1 Investigating Environmental and Internal Conditions

The aim of the first section of SSP is to answer the question *"where are we?"* This requires a comprehensive status analysis. Status analysis essentially covers the following assessments:

- Analysis of the internal structure of the organization (analysis of the duties and authorities, performances, problems, potentials, institutional culture, human resources, technology level, etc., of the organization)
- Environmental analysis (analysis of external conditions as well as the environment in which the organization operates and related parties—target group of the organization and parties affected negatively/positively by the organization's activities)
- Analysis of future developments and their impact on the organization

During and after status analysis, the internal strengths and weaknesses of the business, and the positive and negative developments originating from external factors are identified.

1.1.1 Internal Analysis

When an internal status analysis is performed within the business, the past performance of the business is evaluated and its strengths

5

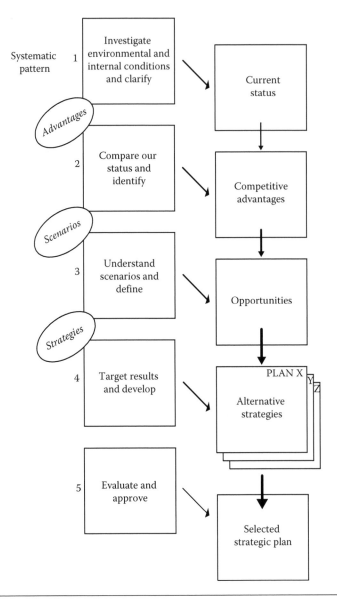

Figure 1.1 SSP—five sections.

and weaknesses are put forth. The purpose is to identify the potential of the business taking into consideration its current performance and problems.

Diagnosing a business' key strengths and weaknesses requires the adoption of a disaggregated view of the business. Examining the business across distinct functional areas is one way to disaggregate the business for internal analysis purposes (*see the Functional Approach form in Chapter 3*).

Therefore, the business should examine past performance (*see the Business History Summary Table in Chapter 3*) to isolate key internal contributors to favorable (or unfavorable) results. What did we do well, or poorly, in marketing operations, and financial operations, and financial management that had a major influence on past results? Was the sales force effectively organized? Were we in the right channels of distribution? Did we have financial resources to support the past strategy? The same examination and questions can be applied to the business' current situation, with particular emphasis on changes in the importance of key dimensions over time.

Quantitative tools cannot be applied to all internal factors, and the judgment of key planners may be used in evaluation. Company or product image and prestige are examples of internal factors more appropriate to qualitative evaluation.

The considerations revealed by Functional Approach are grouped under various functional headings such as overall management, human resources, operations/technology, marketing, finance and accounting, and their distinction as things done well and poorly.

1.1.2 Environmental Analysis

Intention of environmental analysis:

- To determine the developments and trends in the macroeconomical (demographic, economical, judicial–political, technological, sociocultural) environment that effects the business and its industry at most
- To understand the powers that effect competition in the industry (new businesses, customers, suppliers, substitutes, competitors, government, financial institutions, etc.)
- To foresee the trends that these powers would create in the industry

Environmental analysis, which is illustrated in Figure 1.2, considers the general trends in the world, changes in the environment in which the business operates, and particularly the expectations of the group served by the industry. Environmental analysis does not only identify

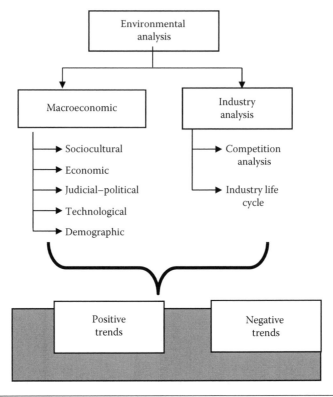

Figure 1.2 Environmental analysis.

the current status but also lays the basis for forecasting the change of scenarios in the future. If a business that is in interaction but cannot control many processes in the environment fails to follow up this change, then strategic planning would not make much sense. Key considerations in environmental analysis are as follows:

- Current global status and development trends in the field of the business
- Current domestic status and development trends in the field of the business
- Critical issues that closely concern the business among the basic trends and problems in the world and in the country; how and in what direction these issues will affect the industry in which the business operates
- Basic negativities and uncertainties faced by the business due to the conditions of the industry

1.1.2.1 Macroeconomic Analysis   Macroeconomic variables are the variables that affect businesses and their industry and are not under the control of businesses. Macroeconomic variables are

- Demographic
- Economic
- Judicial–political
- Technological
- Sociocultural

The variables to be evaluated in order to compose changes and developments are specified later. This review should primarily be conducted at a global scale, and then at regional and country scales.

After collecting information about the present state, efforts must be made to identify trends in variables and the continuation of these trends. The purpose is to ascertain the impacts of variables in the macroeconomic environment on stakeholders.

In order to analyze the effects of trends and developments within these variables on the industry, the *Macroeconomic Analysis form in Chapter 3* can be used. While composing this matrix

- On vertical axis—trends determined on variables
- On horizontal axis—stakeholders of business
- On elements of matrix—the anticipated effects of trends on the stakeholders should be input

The macroeconomic analysis table summarizes the status of the variables with respect to customers', governments', financial institutions', suppliers', shareholders', and employees' points of view. If the macroeconomic factors

- Turn into a better condition, then mark as +
- Remain unchanged, then mark as blank
- Turn into a worse condition, then mark as –

1.1.2.2 Competition Analysis   Porter (1998) stated that if a business is producing a product or service with market considerations like global and domestic market conditions, development/evolution trends of the demand for the subject product and/or service, price movements, changes in quality and standards, competition, etc., are laid down as a result of a comprehensive analysis of the powers in the industry.

The powers that affect a business at most are the groups that create competition within the industry:

- Rivalry among existing companies
- Threat of potential new entrants
- Bargaining power of customers
- Threat of substitutes
- Bargaining power of suppliers
- Bargaining power of other stakeholders (government, trade unions, financial institutions, etc.)

The influence of these powers determines the strength of competition within the industry. In an industry where the power of these groups is high, the potential of profitability will be low. When one of these groups has a higher power, this will have negative implications for the industry, whereas a lower power will have positive implications. Now, let us analyze these powers (*see the Competition Analysis form in Chapter 3*):

Rivalry

Competition in an industry is high if

- The number of active businesses is high
- The growth rate of the industry decelerates or accelerates rapidly
- The characteristics of products/services are not very different
- The fixed costs are high
- The cost of leaving industry is high

Threat of potential new entrants

Entry barriers are high at the rate

- Of having low costs due to the size of the companies within the industry
- Of having brands within the industry
- Of having high investment requirement
- Of accessibility to distribution channels being hard

- Of having high learning curve effect
- Of having various limitations by the government for the new entrants

Bargaining power of customers

Customer is powerful if

- It purchases in large quantities of the products/services of the supplier
- It has the potential of producing products/services by vertical integration
- There are alternative suppliers
- The cost of changing supplier is not high
- It is sensitive to price and service variations
- The purchased product/service does not bear an importance for its production/operation

Threat of substitutes

Substitutes are products/services that cover the same requirements in different ways. In industries where substitutes are plenty and the customers have low product-changing costs, companies can face with less profit.

Bargaining power of suppliers

Suppliers are powerful if

- The industry is composed of limited suppliers
- Their products/services are unique and exclusive
- There is no substitutes in the market
- They have the potential to compete with the current customers through vertical integration
- The purchases compose a small portion of their income

The results of analyses conducted in the light of these and similar considerations will be given in summary (Porter 1998):

- Each force needs to be evaluated in terms of—does it make the market

- High
- Moderate or
- Low attractiveness?
- Each force needs to be evaluated in terms of its relative importance

When the industry changes significantly, it is frequently not because of one competitive force but because of changes to two or possibly three forces combining together (*see Evaluating Competitive Forces and Competitive Forces Status forms in Chapter 3*).

1.1.2.3 Industry Life Cycle   Vernon (1979) stated that each industry passes through the phases of introductory, growth, maturity, and finally regression. The phase that the industry is in facilitates the estimation of impacts and trends of powers defined in competition analysis. Figure 1.3 shows the industry life cycle.

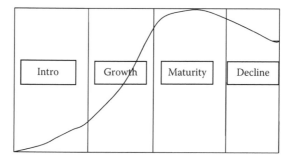

	Intro	Growth	Maturity	Decline
Sales	Low	Rapidly growing	Peak	Declining
Cost	High/customer	Moderate/customer	Low/customer	Low/customer
Profit	Loss	Growing	High	Declining
Competition	Low	Growing	Fixed or declining	Declining

Figure 1.3   Industry life cycle. (Reprinted from Vernon, R., *Oxf. Bull. Econ. Stat.*, 41(4), 255, 1979.)

1.2 Identification of Competitive Advantages

The organization's strengths and weaknesses are compared with the key factors in the market development phases, capacities, and resources of main competitors and the industry's success factors, to identify competitive advantages. Figure 1.4 summarizes the development of a business profile (Pearce and Robinson 2011).

The result of the second section should be a determination of whether key internal factors are as follows (*see the Comparison with Main Competitors and Industry Average and Competitive Advantages—Success Factors—Key Vulnerabilities forms in Chapter 3*):

1. *Competitive advantages*: Factors providing the business with an edge compared to its competitors, and therefore, key factors around which to build the business' strategy.
2. *Basic business requirements*: Factors that are important capabilities for the business to have but are also typical of every

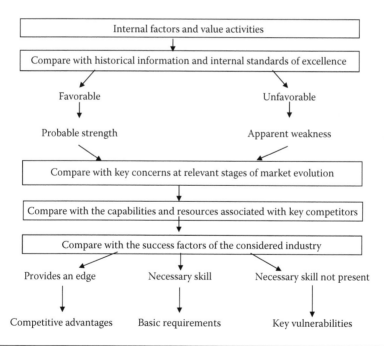

Figure 1.4 Competitive advantages and success factors. (Reprinted from Pearce, J.A. and Robinson, R.B., *Strategic Management: Formulation, Implementation and Control*, McGraw-Hill Higher Education, Columbus, OH, 2011.)

viable competitor; do not represent a potential source of any strategic advantage.

3. *Key vulnerabilities*: Factors on which the business currently lacks the necessary skill, knowledge, or resources to compete effectively. This assessment is also a key input because businesses will want to avoid choosing strategies that depend on factors in this category, and businesses usually target key vulnerabilities as areas for special attention so as to remediate and change this situation.

1.3 Understand Scenarios and Define Opportunities

Figure 1.5 shows the procedure of identifying opportunities.

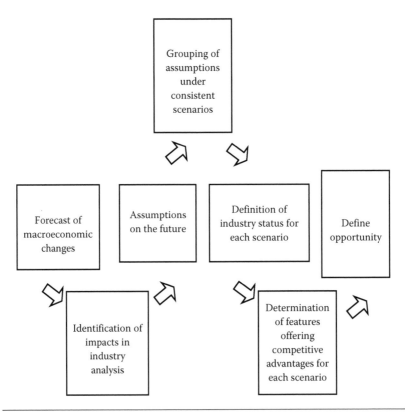

Figure 1.5   Procedure of identifying opportunities.

1.3.1 Scenarios

First of all, the scenarios to be created by trends revealed by environmental analysis for the industry must be developed; that is, alternative scenarios must be developed for the future. Thus, assumptions are grouped under various scenarios, their potential positive and negative impacts on the industry are identified, and the potential status in the industry is defined. Scenarios are as follows:

- Internally consistent views of the future
- Focus on discontinuity and change
- Explore the impact of the change on key players and how they respond to the environment

The opportunities and threats that may be offered and posed for the organization by positive and negative scenarios revealed by scenario analysis must be identified. Furthermore, identification of the organization's competitive advantages and weaknesses relative to competitors and industry standards could lead this section to an efficient result.

In short, in order to identify opportunities and threats, the organization's competitive advantages and weaknesses must be matched with potential positive (attractive) and negative (risky) scenarios that may be encountered in the industry.

1.3.1.1 Assumptions on Future

Assumptions imply the external factors that are not under the direct control of the business preparing the strategic plan but that can affect the progress and success of the strategic plan. After reviewing sociocultural factors, technological factors, political environmental, legal conditions, macroeconomic factors, and variables originating from international system in the environmental analysis, the tendencies of related parties such as competitors, customers, and suppliers must reflect onto the systematic pattern of strategic planning as assumptions.

First, key external variables are identified. Assumptions are made for the values of quantitative and qualitative variables (through brainstorming or statistical models). Brainstorming and/or statistical models are popular estimation techniques:

- Brainstorming is a non numerical estimation technique. While conducting scenario analysis, instruments like participatory meetings bringing together various groups concerning the business are used. For the efforts to be made in this scope, it is possible to outsource specialized services, such as the use of facilitators (moderators) who will neutrally facilitate participatory meetings.
- Statistical models are numerical techniques including relations and other econometric models. However, it is based on historical data, and error margin increases as the structure of relations changes in time.

1.3.1.2 Grouping of Assumptions Position the key assumptions that underpin an issue. Write the assumption in shorthand on a yellow post-it and position relative to others on the grid. Test out relative and absolute positioning (*see the Certainty-Importance Grid in Chapter 3*).

1.3.1.3 Generating Scenarios Generate scenario stories by testing out judgments and identifying interdependencies (*see the Developing Alternative Scenarios form in Chapter 3*):

1. Prepare a list of basic assumptions.
2. Rank the assumptions according to probability of actualization and importance.
3. Convert the classification of each assumption into quantitative values (A = 4, E = 3 ...); multiply the values, and select two or three assumptions with the highest value.
4. Use the selected assumptions individually or as a group to diversify the basic scenario.

1.3.2 Opportunities and Threats

The opportunities and threats that may be offered and posed for the business under the positive and negative scenarios to come out from scenario analysis must be identified. Moreover, determining the strengths and weaknesses of the company compared to its competitors will be able to carry the analysis to a satisfactory result. In short, competitive advantages and weaknesses of the business need to be matched with the potential positive (attractive) and negative (risky) scenarios in the industry.

While developing strategies for the future, opportunities will have a significant influence while threats will be monitored closely by the business and measures will be taken against these threats.

Opportunities, by definition, arise in cases where the unresolved problems and unsatisfied expectations and needs are identified for use of products and/or services in the market, and if solutions can be produced for these.

By testing out total market attractiveness of each positive scenario, you would be able to screen out investment opportunities even before considering what kind of competitive strengths you might be able to attain. The *attractiveness* is the net benefits less the costs (not just the benefits).

Besides market attractiveness of a scenario, to position a business effectively on the GE grid, you also need to take some view of its competitive position with respect to the particular scenario. The following 10 key criteria will usually suffice:

- Brand, image, and reputation
- Simplicity of product/market focus, or alternatively a relevant and broad offering
- Relative market (or niche) share
- Product and service performance
- Distribution channels
- Cost base
- Responsiveness (but this does not mean reactiveness)
- Technical and nontechnical competencies
- Financial strength
- Management skills

The aforementioned factors can be scored as *strong, average, or weak*. Also, the relative importance of the factors can be assessed by weighting some factors as being more important than others. Rasiel (1999) stated that the GE Grid (*see the Business Opportunities form in Chapter 3*) enables you to

- Position a business, having determined market attractiveness of a scenario and competitive position of a business with respect to the particular scenario

- Evaluate business opportunities
- Reposition a business (from right to left on the GE grid, or even [by shifting the business' market focus] diagonally northwest)
- Challenge the adequacy of investment to achieve such a repositioning (both long-term investment and revenue costs with longer-term benefits)
- Compare your positioning with other key competitors operating in the same or different market segments

Not all opportunities are equally valuable. A business with limited resources cannot pursue every opportunity with which it is faced. It must select those opportunities that are going to be the most rewarding. The key decisions in screening and selecting opportunities relate to the size of the opportunity, the investment necessary to exploit it, the rewards that will be gained, and the risks likely to be encountered. Specifically, the decision should be based on the answers to the following questions (*see the Selection of Opportunities—Prioritization form in Chapter 3*):

- *Market attractiveness*: Is the market (or segment) inherently attractive (consider key growth drivers and competitive forces)?
- *Competitive advantage*: Are we likely to have (and be able to sustain) a competitive position?
- *Financial attractiveness*: Are we likely to make enough money out of it?
- *Implementation difficulty*: Do we have the capability, resources, and commitment to implement it effectively?

1.4 Strategic Objectives, Main Goals, and Main Strategies

1.4.1 Strategic Objectives

Strategic objectives are the conceptual results that the business aims at achieving within a certain timeframe. Strategic objectives and main goals answer the question "*what do we want to achieve?*" within the SSP.

1.4.2 Main Goals

Main goals are specific and measurable subobjectives specified for achievement of strategic objectives. Unlike strategic objectives, goals are expressed in quantifiable terms and cover a shorter term. Multiple goals may be established to achieve a strategic objective.

Main goals are the qualitative and quantitative expression of strategic objectives within a defined timeframe (*see the Strategic Objectives—Goals form in Chapter 3*). For this reason, they are measurable subobjectives intended for outputs to be achieved. Goals should be expressed in terms of quantity, cost, quality, and time.

1.4.3 Main Strategies

Strategies are instruments for achievement of long-term goals. It is a course of action selected from a series of options in order to achieve a goal established against uncertainties.

Alternative strategies are developed by searching for an answer to the question "*what should businesses do to be competitive and lasting in their own industries and markets?*"

Determination of a suitable strategy for a business begins in identifying the opportunities and risks in its environment. This (discussion) is concerned with the identification of a range of alternative strategies, the narrowing of this range by recognizing the constraints imposed by business capability, and the determination of one or more strategies at acceptable levels of risk. While evaluating the opportunities defined on the basis of analyses conducted, various strategies we can implement come out:

- You should have a single strategy for a single opportunity.
- If there are multiple opportunities, you can have multiple strategies.

Based on using both the techniques of generic competitive strategies and components of strategy, the main strategy(ies) can be identified. Accordingly, this will lead you to the selection of the corresponding grand strategy(ies.)

1.4.3.1 Generic Competitive Strategies The fundamental basis of above-average performance in the long run is *sustainable competitive advantage*. There are two basic types of competitive advantage a business can possess: low cost or differentiation. Any strengths or weaknesses are ultimately a function of relative cost or differentiation (Porter 1998).

The two basic types of competitive advantage combined with the scope of activities for which a business seeks to achieve them lead to three *generic strategies* for achieving above-average performance in an industry (*see the Generic Competitive Strategies form in Chapter 3*).

Each involves a different route to competitive advantage, combining competitive advantage sought with the scope of the target. The specific actions required for each generic strategy vary widely from industry to industry. Broad target is defined as one that

1. Covers a great diversity of customer needs and market segments
2. Covers a wide and perhaps complex range of products and services
3. Covers both (1) and (2)

1.4.3.2 Components of Strategy In conjunction with its objectives, the firm may choose one, two, or all of the strategy components with respect to its current product-market position (Ansoff 1970). This can be illustrated by means of a matrix (*see the Components of Strategy form in Chapter 3*).

1.4.3.3 Grand Strategies Grand strategies, often called business strategies, provide basic direction for strategic actions. Grand strategies indicate how long-range objectives will be achieved. Thus, a grand strategy can be defined as a comprehensive general approach that guides major actions:

• Are we going to stay in the same ring of value chain? Are we going to continue doing the same work with the same system? (Constancy.)

- Are we going to enter new business areas with additional functions, products, and/or markets? (Expansion.)
- Are we going to leave the business completely? Are we going to leave some of the business? (Reduction.)

Any of the 12 principal grand strategies (Pearce and Robinson 2011) serves as the basis for achieving major long-term objectives of a business, identified according to the techniques of generic competitive strategies and components of strategies:

- Concentration
- Market development
- Product development
- Innovation
- Horizontal integration
- Vertical integration
- Joint venture
- Concentric diversification
- Conglomerate diversification
- Retrenchment/turnaround
- Divestiture
- Liquidation

2

SAMPLE OUTLINE FOR STRATEGIC PLAN

A good strategic plan is between 25 and 50 pages long and takes at least 6 months to write:

Vision
Mission
Basic Policies
Executive Summary

This section should summarize the most important subjects of strategic plan and interconnect various sections. Begin with a two-page or three-page management summary of the venture. Include a short description of the business and discuss major goals and objectives. Describe company operations to date, potential legal considerations, and areas of risk and opportunity.

Strategic Plan

1. Status analysis

The status analysis section is expected not to exceed three pages.

Environmental Analysis

This should consider external factors such as demographic, economical, legal–political, technological, and social changes, market dynamics, customer expectations, competitive conditions, strategies and objectives of competitors, suppliers, substitutes, etc.

- Macroeconomic analysis (global, national)
  - Demographic variables
  - Judicial–political variables
  - Economic variables
  - Sociocultural variables
  - Technological variables

- Competition analysis
  - Rivalry
  - Suppliers
  - Customers
  - Substitutes
  - New arrivals
- Industry life cycle

Internal Analysis: Business Strengths and Weaknesses

The phases of evolution experienced by the business from the past till today and the strengths and weaknesses caused by them on your business structure must be mentioned. This should consider such internal factors as labor force, technology, organization and management, operational matters, products and their market positions, and financial characteristics.

2. Competitive advantages, success factors, and weaknesses

3. Scenarios and opportunities

Positive and Negative Scenarios for Industry

The potential positive and negative scenarios for your industry for the next 5 years must be mentioned, taking into consideration the major developments in your respective industry in the country and worldwide.

Business Opportunities and Threats

4. Strategic objectives, main goals, and grand strategies

The goals intended to be achieved during the next 5 years must be mentioned for each year, taking into consideration the following headings:

Strategic Objectives

Main Goals

- Financial and marketing goals:
  - Which countries to be in
  - Regional concentration
  - Planned strategic partnerships
  - Alliances, merging and acquisitions, etc.
  - Market goals
  - Financial goals, etc.

- Operational goals:
  - Technological improvements
  - Organization, etc.

Grand Strategies

Appendix
Provide a bibliography of all the reference materials you consulted.

3

WORKING FORMS

This chapter contains the forms used for systemic strategic planning (SSP). They may be used when solving your next strategic planning problem. You may copy these forms for your own use, provided you recognize their original source and hold their use within the copyright restrictions covering this book. Each of the forms included in this section is explained in the text and is listed in its order of appearance in the text.

FORM CODE	FORM TITLE
IMECO-SSP-BH1	Business History Summary Table
IMECO-SSP-FA1	Internal Analysis—Functional Approach
IMECO-SSP–ME1	Macroeconomic Analysis Form
SSP-CA1	Competition Analysis Form
SSP-IF1	Evaluating Competitive Forces
SSP-FS1	Competitive Forces Status
IMECO-SSP-CC1	Comparison with Competitors and Industry Average
IMECO-SSP-CW1	Competitive Advantages-Success Factors—Key Vulnerabilities
SSP-CI1	Certainty–Importance Grid
IMECO-SSP-DS1	Developing Alternative Scenarios
SSP-BO1	Business Opportunities
IMECO-SSP-SO1	Selection of Opportunities—Prioritization
IMECO-SSP-OG1	Strategic Objectives—Goals
SSP-CS1	Components of Strategy
SSP-GS1	Generic Competitive Strategies

Business History Summary Table

Prepared by: _____ Business: _____

Authorized by: _____ Project: _____ Date: _____.

	Year	Year	Year	Year	Year	Year
PERSONNEL						
TECHNICAL						
ORGANIZATION and GENERAL MANAGEMENT						
PRODUCTION / OPERATIONS						
MARKETING						
FINANCE and ACCOUNTING (x1000)						

IMECO - SSP – BH1

Functional Approach

Prepared by: _____ .Business: _____ .

Authorized by: _____ Project: _____ Date: _____

	FACTORS	Strengths/Weaknesses
MARKETING	Firm's products /services; breadth of product line	
	Concentration of sales in a few products or to a few customers	
	Ability to gather needed information about markets	
	Market share or submarket shares	
	Product / service mix and expansion potential	
	Channels of distribution: number, coverage and control	
	Effective sales organization	
	Product / service image, reputation and quality	
	Imaginative, efficient and effective sales promotion and advertising	
	Pricing strategy and pricing flexibility	
	Procedures for digesting market feedback and developing new products, services or markets	
	After-sale service and follow up	
	Goodwill/brand loyalty	
FINANCE AND ACCOUNTING	Ability to raise short-term capital	
	Ability to raise long-term capital: debt/equity	
	Corporate-level resources	
	Cost of capital relative to industry and competitors	
	Tax considerations	
	Relations with owners, investors and stockholders	
	Leverage positions	
	Cost of entry and barriers to entry	
	Price-earnings ratio	
	Working capital; flexibility of capital structure	
	Effective cost control, ability to reduce costs	
	Financial size	
	Efficient and effective accounting system for cost, budget and profit planning	
PRODUCTION/ OPERATIONS/ TECHNICAL	Raw materials cost and availability	
	Inventory control systems; inventory turnover	
	Location of facilities; layout and utilization of facilities	
	Economies of scale	
	Technical efficiency of facilities and utilization of capacity	
	Effective use of subcontracting	
	Degree of vertical integration, value added and profit margin	
	Efficiency and cost / benefit of equipment	
	Effective operation control procedures	
	Cost and technological competencies relative to industry and competitors	

	Functional Approach (*continued*)	
	Research and development/technology/innovation	
	Patents, trademarks and similar legal protection	
PERSONNEL	Management personnel	
	Employees' skill and morale	
	Labor relations compared to industry and competition	
	Efficient and effective personnel policies	
	Effective use of incentives to motivate performance	
	Ability to level peaks and valleys of employment	
	Employee turnover and absenteeism	
	Specialized skills	
	Experience	
ORGANIZATION AND GENERAL MANAGEMENT	Organizational structure	
	Firm's image and prestige	
	Firm's record for achieving objectives	
	Organization of communication system	
	Overall organizational control system	
	Organizational climate, culture	
	Use of systematic procedures and techniques in decision making	
	Top-management skill, capacities and interest	
	Strategic planning system	
	Intraorganizational synergy	

IMECO - SSP – FA1

Macro-Economic Analysis Form

Prepared by: _____ Business: _____.

Authorized by: _____ Project: _____ Date:_____.

	DEMOGRAPH					ECONOMICAL								JUDICIAL - POLITICAL					TECHNOLOGICAL					SOCIO - CULTURAL			
	Population growth	Age pattern	Immigration trends	Birth and death ratios	Education level	Change in GDP	Income distribution	Interest rates	Supply of cash	Inflation rate	Unemployment rate	Foreign exchange policy	Saving&consuming trends	Tax laws	Antitrust law	Incentives	Green laws	Business law	Political stability	R&D expenditures	Innovation opportunities	New products	Acceleration - tech. change	Fastness product supply	Increase in automation	Changes in life styles	Expectancy for career	Change in family structure	Changes in personal values
CUSTOMERS																													
GOVERNMENT																													
FINANCIAL INSTITUTIONS																													
SUPPLIERS																													
SHARE HOLDERS																													
EMPLOYEES																													
RESULT																													

+	Change for the better
	Same as before
-	Change for the worse

IMECO - SSP - ME1

Competition Analysis Form

Prepared by:_____ Business: _____.

Authorized by:_____ Project: _____ Date:_____

	FIRMS IN THE INDUSTRY					THREATS OF NEW COMPANIES						COMPETITIVE POWER OF CUSTOMERS						COMPETITIVE POWER OF SUPPLIERS				
	Quantity of firms in the industry	Growth rate of the industry	Differences and the specialties of the products	Fixed costs	Cost to leave the industry	Costs of the companies in the industry related with the company size	Firms which have the customer-firm loyalty	The equity needed to enter the industry	Ability to reach channel of distribution	Cost advantage related with experience	Barriers to enter the industry	The share of the customer in the whole sale	Potential of production of the products by integration	Alternative suppliers	Cost of the change of the suppliers	Flexibility in the prices	The importance of the product for the customers	Quantity of firms in the industry and the production place	Unique products sale	Substitute goods in the market	Potential of production of the products by integration	The share of the sale of the supplier
Low																						
Avg.																						
High																						

SSP – CA1

Evaluating Competitive Forces

Prepared by: _____ . Business: _____ .

Authorized by: _____ Project: _____ Date: _____ .

	FAVORABLE	NEUTRAL	UNFAVORABLE
VERY IMPORTANT	◯		
MODERATE		◯	
	◯		◯
UNIMPORTANT	◯		

SSP – IF1

Competitive Forces Status

Prepared by:_____ .Business: _____.

Authorized by:_____Project: _____ Date:_____.

ENTRANTS

SUPPLIER   RIVALRY   BUYER

SUBST.

✓✓   Very favorable
✓   Neutral

SSP – FS1

Comparison with Competitors and Industry Average

Prepared by:_____ . Business: _____ .

Authorized by:_____Project: _____ Date:_____ .

	FACTORS	OUR BUSINESS	MAIN COMPETITOR(S)	INDUSTRY
MARKETING	Firm's products /services; breadth of product line			
	Concentration of sales in a few products or to a few customers			
	Ability to gather needed information about markets			
	Market share or submarket shares			
	Product / service mix and expansion potential			
	Channels of distribution: number, coverage and control			
	Effective sales organization			
	Product / service image, reputation and quality			
	Imaginative, efficient and effective sales promotion and advertising			
	Pricing strategy and pricing flexibility			
	Procedures for digesting market feedback and developing new products, services or markets			
	After-sale service and follow up			
	Goodwill/brand loyalty			
FINANCE AND ACCUONTING	Ability to raise short-term capital			
	Ability to raise long-term capital: debt/equity			
	Corporate-level resources			
	Cost of capital relative to industry and competitors			
	Tax considerations			
	Relations with owners, investors and stockholders			
	Leverage positions			
	Cost of entry and barriers to entry			
	Price-earnings ratio			
	Working capital; flexibility of capital structure			
	Effective cost control, ability to reduce costs			
	Financial size			
	Efficient and effective accounting system for cost, budget and profit planning			

Comparison with Competitors and Industry Average (*continued*)			
PRODUCTION/TECHNICAL	Raw materials cost and availability			
	Inventory control systems; inventory turnover			
	Location of facilities; layout and utilization			
	Economies of scale			
	Technical efficiency of facilities and utilization of capacity			
	Effective use of subcontracting			
	Degree of vertical integration, value added and profit margin			
	Efficiency and cost / benefit of equipment			
	Effective operation control procedures			
	Cost and technological competencies relative to industry and competitors			
	Research and development/technology/innovation			
	Patents, trademarks and similar			
PERSONNEL	Management personnel			
	Employees' skill and morale			
	Labor relations compared to industry and competition			
	Efficient and effective personnel policies			
	Effective use of incentives to motivate performance			
	Ability to level peaks and valleys of employment			
	Employee turnover and absenteeism			
	Specialized skills			
	Experience			
ORGANIZATION OF GENERAL MANAGEMENT	Organizational structure			
	Firm's image and prestige			
	Firm's record for achieving objectives			
	Organization of communication system			
	Overall organizational control system			
	Organizational climate, culture			
	Use of systematic procedures and techniques			
	Top-management skill, capacities and interest			
	Strategic planning system			
	Intraorganizational synergy			

IMECO - SSP – CC1

Competitive Advantages—Success Factors—Key Vulnerabilities

Prepared by: _____ Business: _____.

Authorized by: _____ Project: _____ Date:_____.

	FACTORS	COMP. ADVANTAGES	SUCCESS FACTORS	KEY WEAKNESSES
MARKETING	Firm's products /services; breadth of product line			
	Concentration of sales in a few products or to a few customers			
	Ability to gather needed information about markets			
	Market share or submarket shares			
	Product / service mix and expansion potential			
	Channels of distribution: number, coverage and control			
	Effective sales organization			
	Product / service image, reputation and quality			
	Imaginative, efficient and effective sales promotion and advertising			
	Pricing strategy and pricing flexibility			
	Procedures for digesting market feedback and developing new products, services or markets			
	After-sale service and follow up			
	Goodwill/brand loyalty			
FINANCE AND ACCUONTING	Ability to raise short-term capital			
	Ability to raise long-term capital: debt/equity			
	Corporate-level resources			
	Cost of capital relative to industry and competitors			
	Tax considerations			
	Relations with owners, investors and stockholders			
	Leverage positions			
	Cost of entry and barriers to entry			
	Price-earnings ratio			
	Working capital; flexibility of capital structure			
	Effective cost control, ability to reduce costs			
	Financial size			
	Efficient and effective accounting system for cost, budget and profit planning			

	Competitive Advantages—Success Factors—Key Vulnerabilities (*continued*)			
PRODUCTION/TECHNICAL	Raw materials cost and availability			
	Inventory control systems; inventory turnover			
	Location of facilities; layout and utilization			
	Economies of scale			
	Technical efficiency of facilities and utilization of capacity			
	Effective use of subcontracting			
	Degree of vertical integration, value added and profit margin			
	Efficiency and cost / benefit of equipment			
	Effective operation control procedures			
	Cost and technological competencies relative to industry and competitors			
	Research and development/technology/innovation			
	Patents, trademarks and similar			
PERSONNEL	Management personnel			
	Employees' skill and morale			
	Labor relations compared to industry and competition			
	Efficient and effective personnel policies			
	Effective use of incentives to motivate performance			
	Ability to level peaks and valleys of employment			
	Employee turnover and absenteeism			
	Specialized skills			
	Experience			
ORGANIZATION OF GENERAL MANAGEMENT	Organizational structure			
	Firm's image and prestige			
	Firm's record for achieving objectives			
	Organization of communication system			
	Overall organizational control system			
	Organizational climate, culture			
	Use of systematic procedures and techniques			
	Top-management skill, capacities and interest			
	Strategic planning system			
	Intraorganizational synergy			

IMECO - SSP – CW1

Certainty–Importance Grid

Prepared by:_____ .Business:_____.

Authorized by:_____Project:_____ Date:_____.

	VERY CERTAIN	UNCERTAIN
VERY IMPORTANT		
LOW IMPORTANCE		

SSP – CI1

Developing Alternative Scenarios

Prepared by:_____ .Business: _____.

Authorized by:_____Project: _____ Date:_____.

POSSIBLE FUTURE UNCERTAINTIES	Degree of Importance (a)	Likelihood-Occurrence (b)	Resultant Score (a)*(b)	To Be Considered

RATING DESCRIPTION

A	Abnormal Impact / Almost Certain to Occur (4)	O	Ordinary Impact / Only Small Likelihood (1)
E	Especially High Impact / Especially Likely to Occur (3)	U	Unimportant / Unlikely (0)
I	Important / Inclined to Occur (2)		

IMECO – SSP – DS1

Business Opportunities

Prepared by: _____ .Business: _____ .

Authorized by: _____ Project: _____ Date:_____ .

	STRONG	MEDIUM	WEAK
HIGH	BIG BANG	Sunrise	Eclipse
MEDIUM	Milky Way	Neutral Zone	White Dwarf
LOW	Red Giant	Sunset	Blackhole

SCENARIO MARKET ATTRACTIVENESS

STRONG   MEDIUM   WEAK

⟵ COMPETITIVE POSITION

SSP – BO1

Selection of Business Opportunities—Prioritization

Prepared by:_____ .Business: _____.

Authorized by:_____Project: _____ Date:_____.

IMPLEMENTATION CAPABILITY	FINANCIAL ATTRACTIVENESS			
	Very High	High	Moderate	Low
A-Absolutely Capable				
E-Especially Capable				
I-Capable				
O-Very Little				
U-Uncertain				
X-Not Applicable				

The diameter of circle represents the relative position of an opportunity w.r.t. the market attractiveness and competitive position of it.

IMECO - SSP - SO1

Strategic Objectives—Goals

Prepared by:_____ .Business: _____ .

Authorized by:_____Project: _____ Date:_____ .

Opportunity

Strategic Objective

	GOAL	Description
FINANCIAL and MARKET	Target markets	
	Product range	
	Sales volume and profitability for the planned period	
	Comparative growth expectations	
	Countries to operate in	
	Regional concentration	
	Strategic partnerships considered	
OPERATIONAL/PERSONNEL/ MANAGEMENT	Organization	
	Training and experience	
	Wage and compensation	
	Investment goals	
	Labor turnover rate	

Strategic Objectives—Goals (*continued*)	
Safety regulations	
Environmental standards	
Technology and equipment choice	
Scrap rates	
Maintenance and repair policies	
Product standards	
Long-term capacity plans	
Production quantities	
Labor level	
Inventory level	
Overtime work	
Subcontractor	

IMECO - SSP - OG1

Components of Strategy

Prepared by:_____ .Business: _____.

Authorized by:_____Project: _____ Date:_____.

PRODUCT		MARKET	
		NEW	**EXISTING**
	NEW	DIVERSIFICATION	PRODUCT DEVELOPMENT
	EXISTING	MARKET DEVELOPMENT	MARKET PENETRATION

SSP – CS1

Generic Competitive Strategies

Prepared by: _____, Business: _____,

Authorized by: _____Project: _____ Date:_____,

	COMPETITIVE ADVANTAGE	
	COST	**DIFFERENTIATION**
SCOPE — **BROAD**	COST LEADERSHIP	DIFFERENTIATION
NARROW	COST FOCUSING	DIFFERENTIATION FOCUSING

SSP – GS1

PART II
CASE STUDIES

Most of the case studies presented in the following chapters are entrepreneurial and new businesses. The data that are used and shown in many cases are fictitious and only help for the purposes of the cases.

Though the cases do not use all the sections/steps and/or techniques of systematic strategic planning (SSP), they still reflect the basics of a typical strategic plan. Though the majority of the cases follow the pattern of SSP methodology and its techniques, some only use the pattern but not the recommended techniques.

In this Part, heading numbers should not be considered as the sections/steps of the systematic process. These numbers are used only for the convenience of structuring the book.

Visual Co.
CGA Technologies
Tchibo
Life...to Go!
Natural Food
Speedy
Unified Tracking Solutions
Abler by Robomedika
Schneider Electric

4
VISUAL CO.*

Vision

To become a totally respected regional company for those looking for breathing space and/or trying to carry themselves to a better mood by capturing and influencing the imagination.

Mission

To be a continual challenger against the leaders of the entertainment industry and make the consumers' moods better by sensorial joy assets.

4.1 Internal Analysis

Table 4.1 shows the functional approach worksheet. In the table,

- The strengths are marked as (+)
- The weaknesses are marked as (–)

4.2 Environmental Analysis

4.2.1 Macroeconomic Analysis

Table 4.2 shows the macroeconomic analysis table that summarizes the status of the variables with respect to customers', governments', financial institutions', suppliers', shareholders', and employees' points of view. If the macroeconomic factor will

- Turn into a better condition, then mark as +
- Remain unchanged, then mark as blank
- Turn into a worse condition, then mark as –

---

* This case study was contributed by Emre Yılmaz, Evrim Varan, and Sinan Dibakoğlu.

Table 4.1 Functional Approach Worksheet

		STRENGTHS/ WEAKNESSES
Marketing	Firm's products/services; breadth of product line	+
	Concentration of sales in a few products or to a few customers	−
	Ability to gather needed information about markets	−
	Market share or submarket shares	−
	Product/service mix and expansion potential	+
	Channels of distribution: number, coverage, and control	−
	Effective sales organization	+
	Product/service image, reputation, and quality	+
	Imaginative, efficient, and effective sales promotion and advertising	−
	Pricing strategy and pricing flexibility	−
	Procedures for digesting market feedback and developing new products, services, or markets	+
	After-sale service and follow-up	−
	Goodwill/brand loyalty	−
Finance and accounting	Ability to raise short-term capital	+
	Ability to raise long-term capital: debt/equity	−
	Corporate-level resources	−
	Cost of capital relative to industry and competitors	−
	Tax considerations	−
	Relations with owners, investors, and stockholders	+
	Leverage positions	+
	Cost of entry and barriers to entry	+
	Price-to-earnings ratio	+
	Working capital; flexibility of capital structure	−
	Effective cost control, ability to reduce costs	+
	Financial size	−
	Efficient and effective accounting system for cost, budget, and profit planning	+

(*Continued*)

Table 4.1 (*Continued*)   Functional Approach Worksheet

		STRENGTHS/ WEAKNESSES
Production/ operations/ technical	Raw materials cost and availability	−
	Inventory control systems; inventory turnover	−
	Location of facilities; layout and utilization of facilities	+
	Economies of scale	−
	Technical efficiency of facilities and utilization of capacity	−
	Effective use of subcontracting	+
	Degree of vertical integration, value added, and profit margin	+
	Efficiency and cost/benefit of equipment	+
	Effective operation control procedures	+
	Cost and technological competencies relative to industry and competitors	−
	Research and development/technology/innovation	+
	Patents, trademarks, and similar legal protection	+
Personnel	Management personnel	+
	Employees' skill and morale	−
	Labor relations compared to industry and competition	+
	Efficient and effective personnel policies	+
	Effective use of incentives to motivate performance	+
	Ability to level peaks and valleys of employment	+
	Employee turnover and absenteeism	+
	Specialized skills	+
	Experience	−
Organization and general management	Organizational structure	+
	Firm's image and prestige	+
	Firm's record for achieving objectives	+
	Organization of communication system	+
	Overall organizational control system	+
	Organizational climate, culture	+
	Use of systematic procedures and techniques in decision making	−
	Top-management skill, capacities, and interest	+
	Strategic planning system	+
	Intraorganizational synergy	+

Table 4.2 Macroeconomic Analysis Table

	DEMOGRAPH						ECONOMIC							JUDICIAL–POLITICAL						TECHNOLOGICAL						SOCIOCULTURAL			
	Population Growth	Age Pattern	Immigration Trends	Birth and Death Ratios	Education Level	Change in GDP	Income Distribution	Interest Rates	Supply of Cash	Inflation Rate	Unemployment Rate	Foreign Exchange Policy	Saving Consuming Trends	Tax Laws	Laws against Monopolization	Incentives	Green Laws	Business Law	Political Stability	R&D Expenditures	Innovation Opportunities	New Products	Acceleration - tech. Change	Fastness Product Supply	Increase in Automation	Changes in Lifestyles	Expectancy for Career	Change in Family Structure	Changes in Personal Values
Customers	+	+	+	+	+		−	−	−	−	+	−	+	−	+	+	+	+		+	+	+	+	+	+	+	+	−	−
Government	+	−	−	+	+		−	+	−	−	−	+	+		+	+	+	+	+	+	+	+	+	+	+		+	+	+
Financial institutions	+	−	+	+	−	+		−	+	−	−		+	+	+	+	+		+	+	+	+	+	+	+	+	+		
Suppliers	+	−	+	+	+		−	+	−	−	−	+	+	−	+	+	+	−	+	+	+	+	+		+	+		+	+
Shareholders	−			+	+	+	+	−	−	−		+	+	−		+	+	+		+	+	+	+	+	+	+	+	+	+
Employees	−	−	−	−	−	+	−	+	−	−	−	−	+	−	+	+	+	+	−	+	+	+	−	−	−		−	−	−
Result																													

+, change for the better; −, change for the worse; same as before.

Customers' point of view

- Demographic and technological factors will change in a better way.
- Economic factors, except unemployment rate and saving/consuming trends, will be worse.
- Gross domestic product (GDP) will be stable.
- Legal and political factors, except tax laws, will be better, and there will be political stability.
- Sociocultural factors, such as lifestyles and career expectancy, will be better.
- Family structures and personal values/beliefs will remain unchanged.

Governments' point of view

- Demographic factors, except age pattern and immigration trends, will be better.
- Economic factors, except interest rates, foreign exchange policy, and saving/consuming trends, will be worse.
- GDP will remain unchanged.
- Legal and political factors, except tax laws and technological factors, will be better.
- There will be no change in tax laws.
- Sociocultural factors, such as family structures and personal values/beliefs, will be worse.
- Lifestyles will remain unchanged.

Financial institutions' point of view

- Demographic factors, except age pattern and education level, will be better.
- Economic factors, except interest rates, inflation rate, and unemployment rate, will be better.
- The foreign exchange policy and income distribution will remain unchanged.
- Legal and political factors, except business law and technological factors, will be better.

- There will be no change in business law.
- All sociocultural factors will be better.

Suppliers' point of view

- Demographic factors, except age pattern, will be better.
- Economic factors, except interest rates, foreign exchange policy, and saving/consuming trends, will be worse.
- GDP will remain unchanged.
- Legal and political factors, except business and tax laws, will be better.
- Sociocultural factors, except career expectancy, will be better.
- Technological factors will be better.

Shareholders' point of view

- Demographic factors, except population growth, will be better.
- Age pattern and immigration trends of the population will remain unchanged.
- Economic factors, except income distribution, foreign exchange policy, and saving/consuming trends, will be worse.
- The unemployment rate and GDP will remain unchanged.
- Legal and political factors, except tax laws, will be better.
- Law against monopolization and political stability will not change.
- All technological and sociocultural factors will be better.

Employees' point of view

- All demographic factors will be worse.
- Economic factors, except GDP, interest rates, and saving/consuming trends, will be worse.
- Legal and political factors, except tax laws and political stability, will be better.

- Technological factors, except research and development expenditures, innovation opportunities, and new products, will be worse.
- Sociocultural factors, except changes in lifestyle, will be worse.

4.2.2 Competition Analysis

Table 4.3 shows the status of the existing firms, threats of new companies, and competitive power of customers and suppliers.

Rivalry

- Number of firms in the industry is few.
- Industry growth rate is uniform.
- Product differences and specialties are high.
- Fixed costs of the firms are high and cost of leaving industry is reasonable.

New players

- High capital investment is necessary to enter into the industry.
- Hard to reach to the channels of distribution.

Customers and suppliers

- Cost of changing suppliers is high.
- Prices are flexible.
- Number of suppliers is few.

4.2.3 Industry Life Cycle

Due to its dependency on technological development, new segments of the media and entertainment industry are constantly being introduced. Entertainment and media is evolved in a highly dynamic nature. Entertainment and media industry revenues were $1,321,890 billion in 2009, and grew further to $1,356,574 billion in 2010, and it is expected to be $1,690,298 billion in 2014 globally.

Internet advertising will be the fastest growing media in the next 5 years. Advertising will increase from $2,005 billion in 2010 to

Table 4.3 Competition Analysis Table

Category	Factor	High	Avg.	Low
FIRMS IN THE INDUSTRY	Quantity of Firms in the Industry	0	0	1
	Growth Rate of the Industry	0	1	0
	Differences and the Specialties of the Products	1	0	0
	Fixed Costs	1	0	0
	Cost to Leave the Industry	0	1	0
THREATS OF NEW COMPANIES	Costs of the Companies in the Industry Related with the Company Size	0	1	0
	Firms Which Have the Customer-Firm Loyalty	0	0	1
	The Equity Needed to Enter the Industry	1	0	0
	Ability to Reach Channel of Distribution	1	0	0
	Cost Advantage Related with Experience	0	1	0
	Barriers to Enter the Industry	0	0	1
COMPETITIVE POWER OF CUSTOMERS	The Share of the Customer in the Whole sale	0	0	1
	Potential of Production of the Products by Integration	0	1	0
	Alternative Suppliers	0	0	1
	Cost of the Change of the Suppliers	1	0	0
	Flexibility in the Prices	0	1	0
	The Importance of the Product for the Customers	0	0	1
COMPETITIVE POWER OF SUPPLIERS	Quantity of Firms in the Industry and the Production Place	0	0	1
	Unique Products Sale	1	0	0
	Substitute Goods in the Market	1	0	0
	Potential of Production of the Products by Integration	0	1	0
	The Share of the Sale of the Supplier	0	1	0

		2009	Increase %	2010	Increase %	2014* (foresight)
Complete entertainment and media industry (trillion $)	Turkey	5,264	11.36	5,862	65.17	9,682
	Global	1,321,890	2.62	1,356,574	24.60	1,690,298
Internet access (billion $)	Turkey	1,457	19.35	1,739	109.20	3,638
	Global	228,060	8.50	247,453	41.88	351,095
Advertising (billion $)	Turkey	1,741	15.16	2,005	57.01	3,148
	Global	405,582	0.91	409,278	21.59	497,648
Consumer/end-user spending (billion $)	Turkey	2,066	2.52	2,118	36.73	2,896
	Global	688,248	1.68	699,843	20.25	841,555

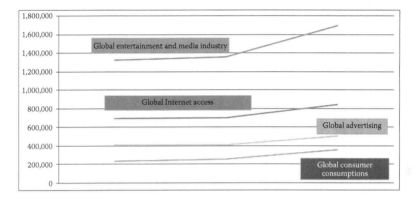

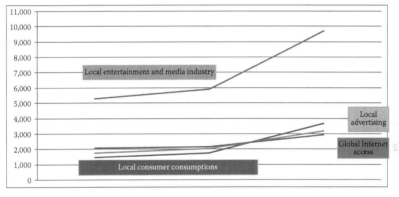

Figure 4.1 Industry life cycle.

$3,148 billion in 2014 in Turkey. Our industry is in a growth stage, as shown in Figure 4.1.

4.3 Competitive Advantages, Success Factors, and Weaknesses

Table 4.4 is a comparison table that ends up with competitive advantages, success factors, and weaknesses of the firm, defined as follows:

Table 4.4   Comparison Table

		INDUSTRY	MAIN COMP.	VISUAL CO.
Marketing	Firm's products/services; breadth of product line	+	+	+
	Concentration of sales in a few products or to a few customers	–	–	–
	Ability to gather needed information about markets	–	–	–
	Market share or submarket shares	+	+	–
	Product/service mix and expansion potential	–	–	+
	Channels of distribution: number, coverage, and control	+	+	–
	Effective sales organization	–	+	+
	Product/service image, reputation, and quality	+	+	+
	Imaginative, efficient, and effective sales promotion and advertising	–	–	–
	Pricing strategy and pricing flexibility	–	–	–
	Procedures for digesting market feedback and developing new products, services, or markets	+	+	+
	After-sale service and follow-up	–	–	–
	Goodwill/brand loyalty	–	–	–
Finance and accounting	Ability to raise short-term capital	–	+	+
	Ability to raise long-term capital: debt/equity	–	+	–
	Corporate-level resources	–	–	–
	Cost of capital relative to industry and competitors	+	+	–
	Tax considerations	–	–	–
	Relations with owners, investors, and stockholders	+	+	+
	Leverage positions	+	+	+
	Cost of entry and barriers to entry	+	+	+
	Price-to-earnings ratio	–	+	+
	Working capital; flexibility of capital structure	–	+	–
	Effective cost control, ability to reduce costs	–	–	+
	Financial size	+	+	–
	Efficient and effective accounting system for cost, budget, and profit planning	–	+	+

(Continued)

Table 4.4 (*Continued*) Comparison Table

		INDUSTRY	MAIN COMP.	VISUAL CO.
Production/ technical	Raw materials cost and availability	−	−	−
	Inventory control systems; inventory turnover	−	−	−
	Location of facilities; layout and utilization of facilities	+	+	+
	Economies of scale	−	+	−
	Technical efficiency of facilities and utilization of capacity	−	−	−
	Effective use of subcontracting	−	−	+
	Degree of vertical integration, value added, and profit margin	+	+	+
	Efficiency and cost/benefit of equipment	+	+	+
	Effective operation control procedures	+	+	+
	Cost and technological competencies relative to industry and competitors	−	+	−
	Research and development/ technology/innovation	−	+	+
	Patents, trademarks, and similar legal protection	+	+	+
Personnel	Management personnel	−	−	+
	Employees' skill and morale	+	+	−
	Labor relations compared to industry and competition	−	−	+
	Efficient and effective personnel policies	+	+	+
	Effective use of incentives to motivate performance	+	+	+
	Ability to level peaks and valleys of employment	−	−	+
	Employee turnover and absenteeism	+	+	+
	Specialized skills	−	+	+
	Experience	−	−	−
Organization and general management	Organizational structure	+	+	+
	Firm's image and prestige	−	+	+
	Firm's record for achieving objectives	+	+	+
	Organization of communication system	+	+	+

(*Continued*)

Table 4.4 (*Continued*) Comparison Table

	INDUSTRY	MAIN COMP.	VISUAL CO.
Overall organizational control system	−	−	+
Organizational climate, culture	+	+	+
Use of systematic procedures and techniques in decision making	−	−	−
Top-management skill, capacities, and interest	−	−	+
Strategic planning system	+	−	+
Intraorganizational synergy	+	−	+

- *Competitive advantages*: Factors providing the business with an edge compared to its main competitor and industry average, that is, the ones that have plus sign only on the Visual Co. column.
- *Success factors*: Factors that are important capabilities for the business to have but are also typical of every viable competitor; do not represent a potential source of any strategic advantage.
- *Key vulnerabilities*: Factors on which the business currently lacks the necessary skill, knowledge, or resources to compete effectively, and shown as minus sign on the Visual Co. column.

4.4 Scenarios and Opportunities

4.4.1 Positive and Negative Scenarios

Positive scenarios

- *Product/service mix and expansion potential*: The industry is new, and yet products are highly demanded.
- *Product/service image, reputation, and quality*: Despite the intensive use of technology, a lot of work is based on creativity, so there will be many opportunities to offer quality products to the market.
- *Ability to raise short-term capital*: Investors are willing to invest in this technology-intensive, promising, and rapidly growing industry.
- Cost of entry and barriers to entry is high for new players.

Negative scenarios

- In media and especially in the animation sector, because of the narrow price range, if costs increase, they cannot be charged to the end user due to the nature of sales agreements.
- The creation of visual products is mainly based on detailed studies, and this may decrease efficiency and increase costs.
- Because of the creativity-based structure and high variety of products, difficulties may arise in using standard procedures and techniques.

4.4.2 Business Opportunity

- Easy to gain a competitive position, as potential entrepreneurs cannot enter into the market due to high cost barriers.
- Cultural richness in the region can be applied to product design and should be used as an opportunity to increase the market share.

4.5 Main Strategies

Within the existing market, our products will always be perceived as creative and new. Product development will be our main strategy, as shown in Figure 4.2.

		Market	
		New	Existing
Product	New	Innovation	Product development
	Existing	Market development	Market concentration

Figure 4.2 Components of strategy.

		Competitive advantage	
		Cost	Differentiation
Scope	Broad	Cost leadership	Differentiation
	Narrow	Cost focusing	Differentiation focusing

Figure 4.3 Generic strategies.

Developing new product features:

- *Adapt*: Know-how will be brought through strategic alliances and will be adapted to the organization. Being a pioneer in the market will be an advantage for substantial product development.
- *Modify*: The technology and theme (characters, soundtracks, etc.) used will be updated according to the market requirements and changing preferences of customers.
- *Minify*: iPhone applications will be created for our trailers integrated with social media.
- *Substitute*: Our products will be applied to the toys of movies, such as animal characters, etc.
- *Combine*: Selling specially designed (logos, themes, shapes) 3D eyeglasses to movie audiences.

We will also focus on differentiation as a strategy, as shown in Figure 4.3, by using our differentiation as a competitive advantage on a narrow scale market.

5

CGA TECHNOLOGIES*

Vision

Make technology invisible for providing total satisfaction for our customers and opportunities for our associates to grow and contribute.

Mission

CGA Technologies is targeting to enhance our customers' businesses by providing consultancy on software and hardware development for telecom companies in the field of information technology (IT) with its international experience to move to a superior position in the market.

We provide a full range of consultancy services and support to help remove the hassles out of your IT projects.

5.1 Internal Analysis

Strengths

- Firm's products/services; breadth of product line
- Ability to gather needed information about markets
- Product/service mix and expansion potential
- Channels of distribution: number, coverage, and control
- Effective sales organization: knowledge of customer needs
- Product/service image, reputation, and quality
- Pricing strategy and pricing flexibility
- Procedures for digesting market feedback and developing new products or services
- After-sale service and follow-up
- Ability to raise short-term capital

---

* This case study was contributed by Aycan Sezin Çınar, Ceren Geçer, and Gizem Öztürk.

- Ability to raise long-term capital: debt/equity
- Cost of capital relative to industry and competitors
- Relations with owners, investors, and stockholders
- Leverage positions
- Cost of entry and barriers to entry
- Price-to-earnings ratio
- Effective cost control, ability to reduce costs
- Efficient and effective accounting system for cost, budget, and profit planning
- Economies of scale
- Effective use of subcontracting
- Degree of vertical integration, value added, and profit margin
- Efficiency and cost/benefit of equipment
- Effective operation control procedures
- Research and development/technology/innovation
- Patents, trademarks, and similar legal protection
- Management personnel
- Employees' skill and morale
- Efficient and effective personnel policies
- Effective use of incentives to motivate performance
- Ability to level peaks and valleys of employment
- Employee turnover and absenteeism
- Specialized skills
- Organizational structure
- Firm's record for achieving objectives
- Organization of communication system
- Overall organizational control system
- Organizational climate, culture
- Top-management skill, capacities, and interest
- Strategic planning system
- Intraorganizational synergy

Weaknesses

- Concentration of sales in a few products or to a few customers
- Market share or submarket shares
- Imaginative, efficient, and effective sales promotion and advertising

- Goodwill/brand loyalty
- Corporate-level resources
- Tax considerations
- Working capital; flexibility of capital structure
- Financial size
- Inventory control systems; inventory turnover
- Cost and technological competencies relative to industry and competitors
- Labor relations cost compared to industry and competition
- Experience
- Firm's image and prestige
- Use of systematic procedures and techniques in decision making

5.2 Environmental Analysis

5.2.1 Macroeconomic Analysis

Macroeconomic analysis summarizes the status of the variables with respect to customers', governments', financial institutions', suppliers', shareholders', and employees' points of view.

On the *demographic* side, population growth rate has a low impact on the IT business environment.

On the *economic* side, growth rate, interest rate, exchange rate, and inflation rate are the factors that have a high impact on the IT business environment.

On the *political* side, government regulations and policies that have a huge impact on IT operations may include trade and labor laws, tax policies, environmental laws and regulations, trade restrictions, commercial tariffs, and infrastructure and development policies. The degree of political stability also has an important impact on the IT business environment.

On the *technological* side, R&D activities, automation, technology incentives, and rate of change have a high impact on IT operations.

On the *social* side, changes in social trends such as health consciousness, career attitudes, emphasis on safety, and change in lifestyles have a normal impact on the demand for IT services.

Table 5.1 Competition Analysis Table

	FIRMS IN THE INDUSTRY					THREATS OF NEW COMPANIES						COMPETITIVE POWER OF CUSTOMERS						COMPETITIVE POWER OF SUPPLIERS				
	Quantity of Firms in the Industry	Growth Rate of the Industry	Differences and the Specialties of the Products	Fixed Costs	Cost to Leave the Industry	Costs of the Companies in the Industry Related with the Company Size	Firms Which Have the Customer-Firm Loyalty	The Equity Needed to Enter the Industry	Ability to Reach Channel of Distribution	Cost Advantage Related with Experience	Barriers to Enter the industry	The Share of the Customer in the Wholesale	Potential of Production of the Products by Integration	Alternative Suppliers	Cost of the Change of the Suppliers	Flexibility in the Prices	The Importance of the Service for the Customers	Quantity of Firms in the Industry	Providing Unique Products/Services	Substitute Goods in the Market	Potential of Production of the Products by Integration	The Share of the Sale of the Supplier
High	0	1	1	0	0	0	0	0	0	1	0	1	1	0	0	0	1	1	1	0	1	0
Avg.	0	0	0	1	0	1	0	1	1	0	1	0	0	0	0	1	0	0	0	1	0	1
Low	1	0	0	0	1	0	1	0	0	0	0	1	0	1	1	0	0	0	0	0	0	0

5.2.2 Competition Analysis

Table 5.1 shows the competition analysis worksheet that helps us to analyze the status of the existing firms, threats of new companies, and the competitive power of customers and suppliers.

5.2.3 Industry Life Cycle

Our industry is in the growth stage, as shown in Figure 5.1.

5.3 Competitive Advantages, Success Factors, and Weaknesses

Table 5.2 compares the competitive advantages, success factors, and weaknesses of the firm, defined as follows:

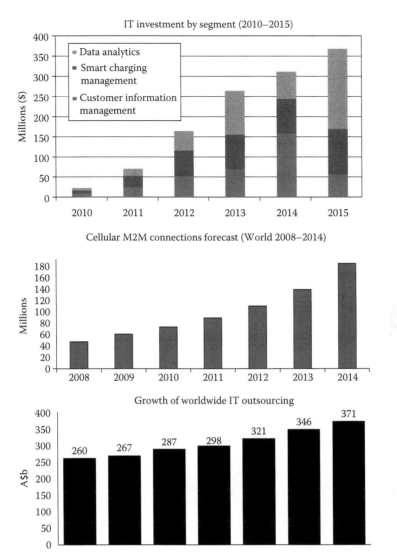

Figure 5.1 Industry life cycle.

- *Competitive advantages*: Factors providing the business with an edge compared to its main competitor and industry average, that is, the ones that have plus sign only on the CGA Tec. column.
- *Success factors*: Factors that are important capabilities for the business to have but are also typical of every viable competitor; do not represent a potential source of any strategic advantage.

Table 5.2   Comparison Table

		INDUSTRY	CGA TEC.	MAIN RIVALRY
Marketing	Firm's products/services; breadth of product line	+	+	+
	Concentration of sales in a few products or to a few customers	−	−	−
	Ability to gather needed information about markets	−	+	+
	Market share or submarket shares	+	−	+
	Product/service mix and expansion potential	−	+	−
	Channels of distribution: number, coverage, and control	+	+	+
	Effective sales organization: knowledge of customer needs	−	+	+
	Product/service image, reputation, and quality	+	+	+
	Imaginative, efficient, and effective sales promotion and advertising	−	−	−
	Pricing strategy and pricing flexibility	−	+	−
	Procedures for digesting market feedback and developing new products or services	+	+	+
	After-sale service and follow-up	+	+	−
	Goodwill/brand loyalty	−	−	−
Finance and accounting	Ability to raise short-term capital	−	+	+
	Ability to raise long-term capital: debt/equity	−	+	+
	Corporate-level resources	−	−	
	Cost of capital relative to industry and competitors	+	+	+
	Tax considerations	−	−	−
	Relations with owners, investors, and stockholders	+	+	+
	Leverage positions	+	+	+
	Cost of entry and barriers to entry	+	+	−
	Price-to-earnings ratio	−	+	+
	Working capital; flexibility of capital structure	−	−	+
	Effective cost control, ability to reduce costs	−	+	−
	Financial size	+	−	+
	Efficient and effective accounting system for cost, budget, and profit planning	−	+	+

(*Continued*)

Table 5.2 (*Continued*) Comparison Table

		INDUSTRY	CGA TEC.	MAIN RIVALRY
Production/ technical	Inventory control systems; inventory turnover	−	−	−
	Economies of scale	−	+	+
	Effective use of subcontracting	−	+	+
	Degree of vertical integration, value added, and profit margin	+	+	+
	Efficiency and cost/benefit of equipment	+	+	+
	Effective operation control procedures	+	+	+
	Cost and technological competencies relative to industry and competitors	−	−	−
	Research and development/technology/ innovation	−	+	−
	Patents, trademarks, and similar legal protection	−	+	+
Personnel	Management personnel	−	+	+
	Employees' skill and morale	+	+	−
	Labor relations cost compared to industry and competition	−	−	−
	Efficient and effective personnel policies	+	+	+
	Effective use of incentives to motivate performance	+	+	+
	Ability to level peaks and valleys of employment	−	−	+
	Employee turnover and absenteeism	+	+	+
	Specialized skills	+	+	+
	Experience	+	−	+
Organization and general management	Organizational structure	+	+	+
	Firm's image and prestige	−	−	+
	Firm's record for achieving objectives	+	+	+
	Organization of communication system	+	+	+
	Overall organizational control system	−	+	+
	Organizational climate, culture	+	+	+
	Use of systematic procedures and techniques in decision making	−	−	−
	Top-management skill, capacities, and interest	−	+	+
	Strategic planning system	+	+	+
	Intraorganizational synergy	+	+	+

- *Key vulnerabilities*: Factors on which the business currently lacks the necessary skill, knowledge, or resources to compete effectively and shown as minus sign on the CGA Tec. column.

Competitive advantages

- Product/service mix and expansion potential
- Pricing strategy and pricing flexibility
- After-sale service and follow-up
- Effective cost control
- Research and development/technology/innovation

Success factors

- Firm's products /services; breadth of product line
- Ability to gather needed information about markets
- Relations with owners, investors, and stockholders
- Efficient and effective accounting system for cost, budget, and profit planning
- Degree of vertical integration, value added, and profit margin
- Effective use of subcontracting
- Patents, trademarks, and similar legal protection
- Specialized skills
- Organizational structure
- Firm's image and prestige
- Firm's record for achieving objectives
- Overall organizational control system

Weaknesses

- Market share or submarket shares
- Working capital; flexibility of capital structure
- Cost and technological competencies relative to industry and competitors
- Firm's image and prestige
- Use of systematic procedures and techniques in decision making
- Ability to level peaks and valleys of employment
- Concentration of sales in a few products or to a few customers
- Imaginative, efficient, and effective sales promotion and advertising

- Goodwill/brand loyalty
- Corporate-level resources
- Experience
- Tax considerations
- Inventory control systems; inventory turnover
- Cost and technological competencies relative to industry and competitors
- Labor relations cost compared to industry and competition
- Use of systematic procedures and techniques in decision making

5.4 Scenarios and Opportunities

5.4.1 Positive and Negative Scenarios

The concluded positive and negative scenarios are shown in Figures 5.2 and 5.3.

5.4.2 Business Opportunity

The concluded business opportunity for CGA Technologies is shown in Figure 5.4.

5.5 Main Goals and Main Strategies

5.5.1 Main Goals

Financial goals

- Exceed $5 million in the next 10 years
- Increase revenue by 15% annually
- Increase gross profit by 15% annually
- Increase contracts with companies by 10% annually

Operational goals

- Continuously improve operational processes
- Capitalize on physical facilities (location, capacity, etc.)
- Improve organizational structure
- Restructure available resources
- Decrease expenses by 5%
- Improve overall productivity

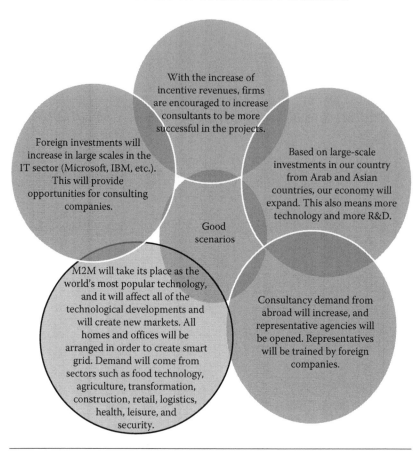

Figure 5.2   Positive scenarios.

5.5.2 Main Strategies

Product development will be the main strategy, as shown in Figure 5.5. This involves investing heavily in research and development for developing new technologies for telecom companies.

CGA Technologies aims to utilize its differentiation advantage for a few selected number of segments in which existing competitors could not meet their requirements. Figure 5.6 shows the selected strategy. CGA Technologies will offer specially tailored software and hardware consultancy to its customers for a premium price.

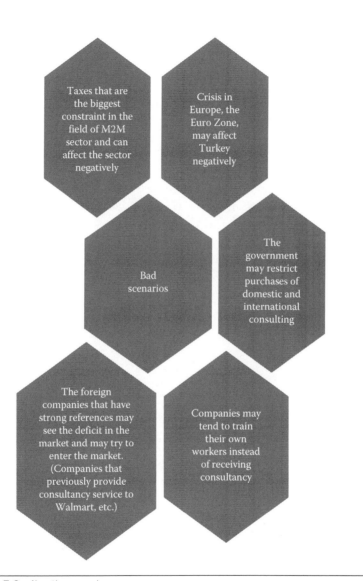

Figure 5.3 Negative scenarios.

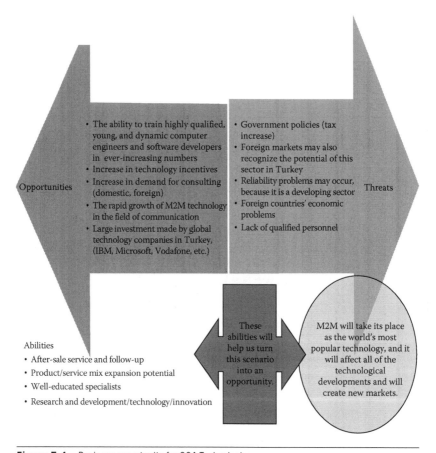

Figure 5.4   Business opportunity for CGA Technologies.

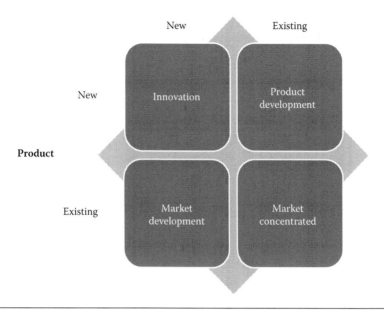

Figure 5.5   Components of strategy.

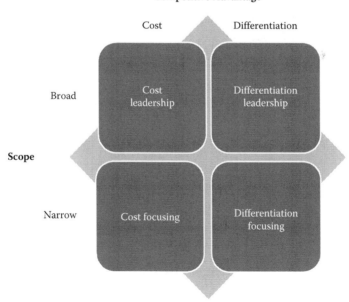

Figure 5.6   Generic strategies.

6
Tchibo*

Tchibo is a retailer of food and nonfood products. The Tchibo shops are a three-in-one-store model, a unique combination of coffee shop, retail store, and coffee bar. The Tchibo shops offer an all-in-one experience. The nonfood product range of Tchibo includes kitchenware to leather jackets. The concept of *every week a new experience* makes the customer curious to look around, experience the new theme, and purchase some useful money-for-value consumer goods.

The primary product that Tchibo has a good reputation with is coffee. The company engaged in distribution of specialized coffee beans. Tchibo sells the products via its website and mail orders and in over 60,000 retail outlets spread across the globe. The company also sells its products at franchise shops and supermarkets. Tchibo has around 40,000 outlets in Germany and 1,300 stores in 60 countries.

In 2006, the company entered the Turkish market by opening its first Turkish Tchibo shop in Europe's largest shopping mall, Istanbul Cehavir. Following a successful market entry, distribution was swiftly expanded to over 30 Turkish shops. There are now Tchibo shops in Germany, the United Kingdom, Austria, Switzerland, Slovakia, Czech Republic, Russia, Poland, Romania, Hungary, and Turkey.

Basic Policies

Our employees are rightly expected to possess a high degree of social and ethical competence. Therefore, as we go about our daily tasks, the following principles serve as a minimum standard of conduct:

- We bear a responsibility to the people in our company. Employee promotion and motivation are very important to us.

---

* This case study was contributed by F. Nur Özen and Y. Koray Karacan.

- People in many different countries trust in the quality, safety, and excellent value for money provided by Tchibo's products. We strive to be worthy of this trust and see customer satisfaction as one of our top priorities.
- Each employee is responsible for ensuring that human rights and fundamental social standards are not violated in their spheres of jurisdiction and influence. This applies, in particular, for working conditions at our suppliers and business partners.
- We see environmentally conscious action not only as a corporate obligation but also as an important condition for sustained, healthy growth.
- We are engaged in community projects in order to improve the social conditions in those countries in which Tchibo does business.
- The implementation and evolution of these values calls for an ongoing critical questioning of one's own position.

6.1 Environmental Analysis

6.1.1 Macroeconomic Analysis

6.1.1.1 Demographic   Turkey has a high population, and this is the third largest population in Europe with about 77 million people. It is slightly growing every year. The greatest part of the population lives and works in the western part of Turkey. Regions of Turkey with the largest populations are Istanbul (+12 million), Ankara (+4.4 million), Izmir (+3.7 million), and Bursa (+2.4 million). An estimated 70.5% of the population lives in urban centers.

6.1.1.2 Judicial–Political   Turkey's constitution governs the legal framework of the country. It sets out the main principles of government and establishes Turkey as a unitary centralized state. Turkey is a member of the United Nations, the OECD, the OIC, the OSCE, the ECO, the BSEC, and the G-20 major economies. In 2008, Turkey was elected as a nonpermanent member of the United Nations Security Council. Turkey's membership of the council effectively began in 2009.

The first domestic franchising in Turkey started with Turyap in 1985, and the first foreign franchising started in 1986 with

McDonald's. Then, the franchisors have especially developed four categories: clothing, real estate, transports, and fast food.

Franchising in Turkey can trust in UFRAD (National Franchise Association): according to some statistical data from UFRAD, there are about 100 franchisors and 1500 franchisees working in Turkey. As there is no specific law to regulate franchise, the agreements between the parties establish directly all the contents in the trade-off and the approval of General Directorate for Foreign Investment (GDFI) is required if the trade-off involves foreign companies. Usually, the royalty is around 5% on-sold for food and beverages, but this percentage is expected to be higher for other categories.

6.1.1.3 Economic

- Exports are $115.3 billion f.o.b. (2007 est.).
- Commodities are apparel, foodstuffs, textiles, metal manufactures, and transport equipment.
- Partners are Germany, 11.3%; the United Kingdom, 8%; Italy, 7.9%; the United States, 6%; France, 5.4%; and Spain, 4.4% (2006).
- Imports are $162.1 billion f.o.b. (2007 est.).
- Commodities are machinery, chemicals, semifinished goods, fuels, and transport equipment.
- Partners are Russia, 12.8%; Germany, 10.6%; China, 6.9%; Italy, 6.2%; France, 5.2%; the United States, 4.5%; and Iran, 4% (2006).

The main goods that Turkey exports are textiles, cotton, clothing, glass, oils and other fuels, iron and steel, precious stones, pearls, tobacco, and foods. Germany, Italy, France, the United Kingdom, and the United States are the leading countries to which Turkey exports bulk of its goods.

The main items that Turkey imports include machinery, iron and steel, aircraft and associated products, mechanical appliances, electrical equipment, and pharmaceuticals. The United States, Italy, Germany, Russia, France, the United Kingdom, and Switzerland are the main countries from where Turkey imports the bulk of the goods.

In order to negate the effects of worldwide recession and reducing figures of its exports to the European countries, Turkey is now looking forward to expanding in new markets. Turkey is now exporting to several countries in the Middle East, Central Asia, and Africa.

There is an observation about Turkey's trade relations that the most intensive one is with Germany in consideration of Turkey's bilateral economic and trade relations with foreign countries. In 2009, Germany imported goods, $14 billion, to Turkish and German states in first rank places as well as in previous years. The most significant product groups traded between Germany and Turkey are *knitted apparel, accessories, machinery, equipment,* and *tools.*

6.1.1.4 Sociocultural   Turks are known as enthusiastic coffee drinkers. Even the formation of culture around coffee and cafés dates back to sixteenth-century Turkey. Cafés in Western Europe and the Eastern Mediterranean were traditionally social hubs. Drinking coffee is the most common social activity for Turks. This is part of the Turkish culture and can be observed in leisure time and during work. Drinking coffee is an accepted form of relaxation and social conduct. Anyhow, the annual per capita consumption of coffee of Turkey in 2008 is 0.4 kg. This is way below Finland, which is 12 kg. But in the last 2 years, according to the growth of the young population and coffee chains, coffee consumption is increasing every day.

6.1.1.5 Technological   Technology is a trend that exists almost in all sectors. It is important for households as well. The demand for functional kitchen utensils and coffee machines is increasing in markets where participants generally need easiness in their daily life.

6.1.2 Competition Analysis

6.1.2.1 Rivalry   There are no direct competitors because Tchibo's concept is unique worldwide due to its special *three-in-one-store* model and the *week* concept. However, the products that Tchibo offers have many indirect competitors.

Starbucks: Starbucks is the largest coffeehouse chain company in the world with more than 15,011 stores in 44 countries worldwide. The Starbucks business concept operates with Starbucks-owned stores and licensed franchise stores. Starbucks keeps expanding to foreign markets: every day an average of seven new Starbucks stores open.

The Starbucks assortment covers different kinds of brewed coffee, espresso, cappuccino, hot and cold drinks, as well as roasted coffee beans, coffee mugs, and other coffee equipment. The snack assortments range from pastry over sandwiches to salads. Starbucks has several joint ventures and therefore licensed locations in airports, theme parks, grocery stores, hospitals, and university campuses. The mission of Starbucks is to create a third place between home and work. In 2003, Starbucks opened the first store in Turkey; today, there are more than 100 stores in Turkey (2009 Starbucks).

Gloria Jean's: Gloria Jean's Gourmet Coffees is one of the largest mall-based retailer of specialty coffees in the world. Their first store opened in 1979. Today, there are over 1000 stores in 40 countries with plans to expand annually. Gloria Jean's Gourmet Coffees serves almost 200 various drinks that are made with special coffee beans. In Turkey, Gloria Jean's has stores in Istanbul, Ankara, Izmir, Eskisehir, and Bursa.

Kahve Dünyası: The number of coffee shops reached 20 stores from Istanbul to Antalya. Its primary product is Turkish coffee. Besides coffee, they also offer handmade chocolates of their own production, which is sold under the name of Chocolate World.

Boyner: Boyner is Turkey's biggest department store chain, with 28 multistores, 11 concepts, and 10 outlet stores nationwide. The company was established in 1981 in Istanbul. The revenues reached 521.5 million TL in 2009. The total sales area was in 2009: 9.588 m². Boyner department stores offer clothing, home furnishing, consumer electronics, household appliances, and more.

YKM: YKM was the first department store in Turkey and was established in 1950. YKM offers all products a family needs, from clothes to cosmetics and personal care products and technological products to electric home appliances and home decoration. YKM caters to the many needs of 35 million visitors per year with its 58 stores in 32 cities, over 4000 employees, more than 1000 providers, over 1100 brands, 150,000 kinds of products, and over 125,000 m² sales area as of 2009. YKM is the only member of IADS (International Association of Department Stores) representing Turkey.

Migros: Migros opened its first store in Beyoğlu at the fish market in 1957. Migros has a total of 1941 stores with 357 Migros, 264 Tansaş, 1.269 Şok, 11 Macro Center, and 10 5M in 73 cities in Turkey and

30 Ramstore stores abroad. In 2009, the revenue was 5,073,746 TL (thousand).

6.1.2.2 Suppliers   Most of the products are produced in China, and the Chinese manufacturer market is highly competitive. This freedom of choosing a producer keeps the bargaining power of the suppliers low.

6.1.2.3 Customers   The current buyers are households in several European countries who are searching for great coffee taste at a fair price and useful value for money. Products are for all ages and income levels. Although the product range is not gender-related, it should be considered that the majority of the buyers will be women because they mostly do the family shopping. Potential buyers could be Turkish households.

Buyers choose products because they look for excellent quality at a fair price. They want great coffee taste and the experience of the *every week a new experience* concept. Consumer goods are for use in daily life. Consumer goods are innovative, creative, and useful and should enrich the life of the customer.

6.1.2.4 Substitutes   Consumer goods and coffee beverages can be bought in many different places. Both of these markets are highly competitive, and the consumer has different options to fulfill their needs.

6.1.2.5 New Arrivals   A few firms control most of the market share and have the power. That makes it relatively difficult for new entrants. However, the franchise sector is growing in Turkey and different concepts from all over the world could be established.

6.1.3 Industry Life Cycle

There are up to 1000 aromas in a single coffee bean that can be released through the roasting process. Each region-specific raw coffee type requires special roasting conditions to develop its individual taste and aroma profile in an optimum way. Specialty coffee is a segment of the coffee industry. This term is used to describe beans of the best flavor that are produced in special microclimates. Specialty coffee is commonly used to refer to gourmet coffee. Specialty coffees are grown in special and ideal climates and are distinctive because of their full cup taste and little to no defects. Their unique flavors and tastes are a result of the special characteristics and composition of the soils in which they are produced.

The specialty coffee segment is the most rapidly growing portion of the coffee industry. In the United States, specialty coffee has increased its market share from 1% to 20% in the last 25 years. To promote and self-regulate the industry, growers, exporters, roasters, retailers, and equipment suppliers have established trade associations. These associations exist in both coffee-consuming and coffee-producing countries.

According to the National Coffee Association, 49% of Americans aged 18 or older drink some type of coffee beverage daily, and many of them wait in lines at specialty coffee retailers to get their fix. The cafe segment of the specialty coffee market, including cafes, kiosks, carts, and coffee bean roaster/retailers, continues to grow. Specialty coffee (Starbucks, Tchibo, etc.) franchises are increasing day by day. Recently, specialty coffee consumption has moved toward the homes, where high-quality whole beans has become an important aspect.

6.2 Internal Analysis

6.2.1 Marketing

6.2.1.1 Sales Channel Tchibo uses a multichannel distribution in order to offer the products and services as convenient as possible for its customers.

Shop in shop (special retail partners): Tchibo has many concession partners and Tchibo products are sold in bakeries, supermarkets, drugstores, tobacco shops, hardware stores, and photo shops. A shop-in-shop concept is used in order to create the right brand awareness. Approximately one-third of all special retail partners offer the *every week a new experience* and a coffee bar service. For each sales outlet, individual sales solutions are developed. Tchibo supports the retail partners with several services, for example, promotion material. Furthermore, a good cooperation with big supermarkets provides Tchibo with a well-spread distribution network.

Direct (*mail order business and e-commerce*): Customers can order nonfood products and the coffee range via the mail order magazine published monthly. The four nonfood themes of the month and the coffee range are represented in the magazine. Moreover, customers can order the coffee range, the current consumer goods of the week and the last 3 weeks, and special offers over the Internet. Tchibo has its own online shops for Turkey, as well as an EU online shop.

6.2.1.2 Products and Services Tchibo offers a combination of coffee and well-priced, quality consumer goods. Tchibo sells two kinds of products.

Food products: The core business of Tchibo is coffee. The coffee expertise and the quality of the brand are well known and appreciated among customers. The coffee range goes from all classic roasted to instant coffees. The tastes vary from decaffeinated to espresso.

Nonfood products: Tchibo has created a worldwide unique and successful concept. Tchibo's idea and slogan is *every week a new experience*. Each week a new theme is created and around this theme Tchibo offers approximately 30 consumer good products that are exclusively made for the company. The themes suit the seasons and complement each other. The weekly changing range of products makes the customers return on a regular basis.

6.2.1.3 Image and Quality Another important core feature is the value for money and quality concept. Tchibo offers good quality at a fair price. Over the years, Tchibo has built a trust relation with their customers. As stated in the mission statement, *Customer satisfaction and living up to the trust our customers place in us are the top priorities of Tchibo*. Tchibo products have high standard in terms of materials, durability, functionality, manufacture, and safety.

All items are exclusively produced for Tchibo. Before the products are offered to their customers, Tchibo makes sure that they comply with Tchibo's safety and quality standards.

6.2.1.4 After-Sale Service Further services, which come with the products, are a 2-year warranty and a 3-year guarantee for technical products and zips, repair or product replacement service, and the right of return.

6.2.2 *Production/Operations*

Tchibo develops some 2000 products a year: footwear, swimwear, clothes, furnisher, stereos, etc. At Tchibo, a team of product managers, buyers, marketing professionals, and quality developers are responsible for the product idea, its planning, and its execution. There is a team for the areas of *bath & home, women's clothing and accessories,* and *children & outdoors.*

Tchibo develops each product and is produced exclusively for itself. Tchibo contracts a make-up manufacturer and takes on the responsibility of distribution from the manufacturer country to its own stores and depots within other stores. The manufacturers of raw materials are subcontractors to the first tier supplier of Tchibo.

The major production countries are currently Bangladesh, China, Pakistan, India, Turkey, Laos, and Vietnam. Then, these products are tested by their in-house testing department as well as by independent laboratories.

6.2.3 *Personnel*

Tchibo employed a total of 8465 employees in 2009, including trainees and management trainees. There are a range of job positions including brand, sales, and marketing manager, of which 5358 were employed part time, mainly in more than 900 shops.

6.2.3.1 Labor Relations Employees at Tchibo are paid strictly according to performance-based criteria as set out in the job requirements.

6.2.3.2 Employee Skill and Training In Tchibo, employees should always be able to cope with increasing demands, thus supporting them with a comprehensive range of further training measures. At Tchibo, they are all constantly required to cope with new challenges. This is where it supports its employees through a personnel development program in order to support the employees actively and help them to recognize and promote their individual potential. The program includes skills training, management development, and foreign languages.

In 2007 and 2008, expenditure on training exceeded €900,000, while in 2009 around €1,100,000 was invested in training and further development for Tchibo employees.

6.2.4 *Finance and Accounting*

As stated in the financial report of 2006, revenues exceeded €9 billion in 2006 for the first time, which is a total increase of 3%. Furthermore, in 2005, the revenues were €4 billion, while in 2006, only €3.9 billion. This is a decline of 2%, which happened due to a highly competitive German market and investments in new business areas.

In 2006, the earnings per share amounted to €178.73; in the previous year, it was €75.70. As the ratio gets higher, the stock value increases. Foreign revenues increased for the Tchibo subgroup by 4%, pushing foreign business as a proportion of total revenues to 23%. This means that the companies' international business branch becomes, to a greater extent, important for Tchibo.

In the final months of 2008 and at the beginning of 2009, worldwide economic activity declined considerably as a result of the financial crisis. Since the third quarter of 2009, the economy in nearly all countries has recorded a slight growth again. As a result of the financial crisis, however, the economy is slow to develop due to adjustment processes in the industrialized countries. The retail sector reported a revenue decline in 2009. Still the effects of the financial crisis on the retail sector were small when compared with other branches of the industry.

6.3 Business Strengths and Weaknesses

Strengths

- Tchibo has a worldwide unique three-in-one-store model and distinctive *every week a new experience* marketing concept
- Company reputation, promotion effectiveness
- Tchibo offers high-quality products at a low price
- Great know-how in the coffee and consumer goods business
- Early adopter of Internet and strong in e-commerce
- Training courses

- Career opportunities
- Product and service quality
- The effects of the financial crisis on the retail sector were small when compared with other branches of industry

Weaknesses

- The concept is not clear for all targets
- Brand image is not known internationally
- Training costs
- Technical manufacturing skill
- Revenue was down from the previous year in 2009
- Financial instability

6.4 Competitive Advantages and Success Factors

Competitive advantages

- *Early adopter of Internet and strong in e-commerce*: Tchibo has an online store. Customers can reach every product with special offers in its food or nonfood products. Tchibo's competitors are not strong enough to reach the level of Tchibo's success in e-commerce. Almost none of them has online stores except its indirect competitors like hypermarkets and department stores.
- *Unique three-in-one-store model*: The nonfood, coffee, and coffee-bar divisions comprise an up-to-date and harmonious three-in-one-store concept. Tchibo's unique store model does not exist in its competitors. For example, Starbucks has coffee and coffee-bar divisions, but it does not have nonfood products except coffee machines. These nonfood products in Tchibo can be fashionable clothes that are attractive for some customers who are willing to pay for clothes during shopping. This is another competitive advantage of Tchibo.
- *Every week a new experience marketing concept*: Tchibo's *every week a new experience* marketing concept serves a very different consumption experience to its customers. Starbucks, other specialty coffee retailers, or any competitor belonging

to the food industry do not focus on this marketing concept. Every week new designs and brand-new nonfood products are ready to be sold on the shelves. Tchibo's special coffees have a lead role each week according to the concept. This marketing concept is very attractive to the customers. This is why it is a major competitive advantage of Tchibo.

Success factors

- Great know-how in the coffee and consumer goods business
- Effective advertising
- Price competitiveness
- Customer loyalty
- Consistency

6.5 Scenarios and Opportunities

6.5.1 Positive Scenarios for Industry

- If there is a possible quota or trade barrier for Turkey, this will decrease production and sales.
- If there is an increase in disposable income of households, sales will increase as well.
- In the long run, due to the increase in the young population, the demand for coffee and nonfood products will increase.
- Growing franchise industry in Turkey.
- Potential growth of Internet technologies and e-commerce will increase the online sales.

6.5.2 Business Opportunities and Threats

Opportunities

- Household income and demand for consumer goods rise.
- Future coffee consumption may increase.
- Turkish franchise industry grows steadily.
- Increasing brand awareness.
- E-commerce has a big growing potential.

Threats

- Several strong indirect competitors
- Sudden macroeconomical changes
- Possible unstable economy of other countries that are related to Tchibo

6.6 Main Goals and Main Strategies

6.6.1 Main Goals

Financial and marketing goals

- Make more investment on advertising
- Increase market share by 7% in the coming years
- Open new stores with lower store-opening costs

Operational goals

- Increasing the share of sustainable coffee. Make new arrangements with other countries that have coffee beans as raw material for new specialized coffee types that are not currently selling in the store.
- Invest more in R&D to develop new products for the *every week a new experience* concept.
- Maintain the social benefits package even in tough economic times.

6.6.2 Main Strategies

Tchibo has a great expertise in the coffee and consumer goods market. Over the years, Tchibo established good business relations with its partners and suppliers; therefore, Tchibo can offer high-quality products at a good price. Besides, there are no direct competitors. A niche could be created in new markets.

Since Tchibo only has little experience in globalization, entry strategy would be via joint venture. Tchibo has great opportunities to offer and a joint venture with local business partners that have experience and great knowledge in local markets can be very beneficial for both business partners.

In existing markets, Tchibo shops are owned by Tchibo or franchisees. The unique three-in-one-store model is excellently marketable as a franchise concept. Besides, Turkish franchise market has a growth potential that gives Tchibo the opportunity with less risk.

Additionally, in order to manage costs and ensure compliance with the company's rigorous standards of freshness, quality, and consistency, the company should control its coffee sourcing, roasting, and retail sales.

7

LIFE...TO GO!*

Life...to go! is an online-based delivery service of what will initially be groceries. It is a service company that allows customers to visit its website, order and purchase their groceries, and then have them directly delivered to their door or to their address of choice. The inventory of grocery products will be provided by the company's partners, which are two supermarkets with a significant market share in the Dutch market and who are direct competitors of the largest supermarket chain in the Netherlands, Albert Heijn (AH).

This partnership allows *Life...to go!* to benefit from an established customer base and well-known brand names and high-quality and service evaluation while providing the partnering supermarkets with a way of competing with AH in the online-delivery service industry without incurring too many additional costs and/or risks (compared to if they started such a venture on their own) and by hopefully capturing a part of that market as well.

The company's target group is busy, on-the-go consumers with little time available in the day to get all their necessary activities done. For many people, this means continually pushing certain activities to the background until the very last minute or until it is too late and that is where *Life...to go!* comes in and offers an easy solution to one of life's everyday chores such as grocery shopping.

Similarly, the consumer segment of the elderly or physically and even perhaps mentally disabled is also a target group for the company. The service does not have to necessarily be provided directly to this segment itself but perhaps to their caregivers as this group of customers also has a lot on their plate. Caregivers can be anyone from family to friends to health-care providers who are paid to take care of those

---

* This case study was contributed by Tianda Windfield and Colinda Dos Santos.

a bit more challenged than others. This service can also help them in their own lives by lightening the chore load after they have punched out from work, but it can also help them during working hours while assisting those they are responsible of taking care of, which might include helping them with grocery shopping.

Mission

Our aim is to provide a one-of-a-kind, efficient, and time-saving online-based delivery service for our customers who have other more time-consuming priorities. Our service has a broad reach that saves our customers time and allows them the space and freedom to conduct their other, more pressing daily activities.

In short, our mission is *to provide an adequate, efficient, and time-saving service for all our customers with quality and a personal touch.*

7.1 Environmental Analysis

7.1.1 Macroeconomic Analysis

7.1.1.1 Demographic   Everyone goes to the supermarket at some point. The Netherlands has approximately 17 million (16,669,112 in 2011) inhabitants, who go to the supermarket an average of two to three times per week in order to meet their most basic needs. A very small amount of those inhabitants utilize the online delivery service of two main providers (discussed in detail in the competitive analysis) of online delivery of groceries.

Dutch residents go to the supermarket an average of two to three times per week, which is quite often. Therefore, it can be assumed that the people who use an online grocery delivery service are usually quite busy during the day (and in their daily lives in general) and thus have no real spare time to go grocery shopping.

7.1.1.2 Judicial–Political   A quarter of consumers have a choice from one or more supermarkets when they need to go grocery shopping. This is because municipalities have no legal means to regulate the establishment of supermarkets, which is a testament to the powerful position of large supermarket chains.

SOMO (Stichting Onderzoek Multinationale Ondernemingen) did earlier research into the increasing power of supermarkets. With regard to the fact that they are increasing, consumers embrace them as suppliers of a wide choice of low prices. This development allows for a dominant position of supermarket chains, at the expense of small grocers.

The current legislation protects supermarkets relative to the aggressive behavior of food producers, which was needed in the past. However, the roles have exchanged. The supermarkets are strong players now, and an outdated legislation places them strategically on the map. Still, supermarkets have generally little to say about legislation and AH, in particular, would like to see a change in this. For example, AH wants a law passed for sustainable products in which the government will force a breakthrough in the market for and of organic and fair trade products.

On another note and with regard to more standard and general legislation, there are generally three laws of food safety: the Consumer Goods Act, the Consumer Goods Act Hygiene Scheme of Foodstuffs, and the Consumer Goods Act Preparation and Handling Scheme of Food; and to ensure food safety, there are also certain procedures such as HACCP and quality standards.

Finally, all supermarkets also have a law on shop opening times; that is, how long supermarkets may stay open and also being open on Sundays, because in the Netherlands, on the last Sunday of the month supermarkets can only be open for a certain amount of time. In addition, there is, of course, the alcohol ban for young people under 16 years of age and identification must also be shown if asked by an employee of the supermarket.

7.1.1.3 Economic In order to take a closer look at the external factors influencing the industry and subsequently the company from an economic standpoint, this section will examine the purchasing power of consumers, which reveals that in 2009 Dutch people had on average 1.4% more to spend than in 2008; however, entrepreneurs and independent (self-employed) people still saw their purchasing power being reduced through sudden sales declines. This is evident from the figures that the Central Bureau of Statistics (in Dutch: Central Bureau voor Statistiek [CBS]) has announced. The slight growth in purchasing power was particularly due to the large number of Dutch people who were employed and that kept their jobs.

The disposable income of that group rose by 3.1%. It was the Dutch independent entrepreneurs who were hard hit in 2009. They saw their turnover plunging and lost on average more than 4% of their purchasing power; that effect was also reflected in higher-income households that earned more than €160,000 gross and who were relatively independent entrepreneurs. They were the only income group that, in 2009, went backward. According to a CBS economist, Muligen, it was very well possible that in 2010 the independent entrepreneurs would be the first to benefit from the recovery that occurred and continues to occur.

At that time, it was predicted that in 2010 and 2011 the purchasing power of the average Dutchman would fall (average wages would decrease) as a result of a delayed effect from the most serious crisis since the 1930s. A similar effect occurred in the period after 2003 when the purchasing power fell, and then again in 2005 when it decreased as a result of a year with weak economic growth.

However, with regard to 2011, it can be said that the purchasing power had risen as consumers' purchase behavior was becoming more expensive due to the soaring prices of commodities (food items are quickly becoming expensive). This is an approximate 30% rise based on research firm GfK—short for Society for Consumer Research. In June 2011, the prices increased by another 3%, which was higher than the previous year. As a result, consumers are now massively purchasing differently according to Joop Holla (GfK), they go to cheaper supermarkets, they choose less well-known brands (A-brands), or they choose substitute products.

7.1.1.4 Sociocultural   For sociocultural factors in the supermarket industry, the focus will mainly be on the current lifestyles of customers in the current economic situation and what is *in* at the moment. A sustainable diet (healthy lifestyle) is the newest trend for customers to engage in, and they expect to see supporting products in the supermarkets. Consumers are increasingly buying organic (products), and especially for fresh products (such as produce), consumers like to buy the biological alternative.

Also, the typical traditional supermarket is slowly disappearing. The future belongs to the hypermarket and the small city grocers, where assortment is strongly extended. It is also predicted that the traditional distinction will fade between discounters (such as Aldi, Lidl, and Dirk van den Broek) with low prices and a limited supply, on the one hand, and with *luxury* supermarkets such as AH and Super de Boer with higher prices, a wide assortment and lots of fresh products, on the other hand. An overview of all mega supermarkets (i.e., supermarkets larger than 2500 m²) in the Netherlands is shown in Figure 7.1.

Together with the CBL annual report, the researched consumer trends were also announced; this was a large national research focused on what consumers currently think about supermarkets. The research revealed that although 97% of the Dutch population believes that the supermarkets respond to their wishes, they still have additional needs that can be seen next. However, consumers gave the supermarkets an average report rate of 7.7.

Supermarkets >2500 m² v.v.o. in the Netherlands

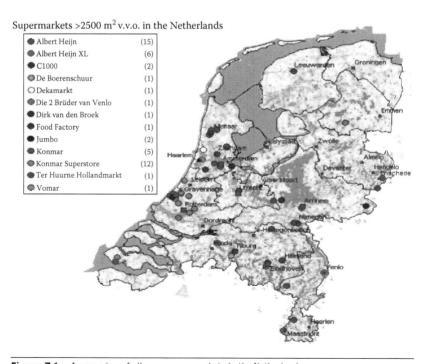

● Albert Heijn	(15)
● Albert Heijn XL	(6)
● C1000	(2)
◐ De Boerenschuur	(1)
○ Dekamarkt	(1)
● Die 2 Brüder van Venlo	(1)
● Dirk van den Broek	(1)
● Food Factory	(1)
● Jumbo	(2)
● Konmar	(5)
◐ Konmar Superstore	(12)
● Ter Huurne Hollandmarkt	(1)
◐ Vomar	(1)

Figure 7.1 An overview of all mega supermarkets in the Netherlands.

The CBL needs the following top five looks:

1. Quick cashiers (84%)
2. ATMs (72%)
3. Pinning extra money at checkout (cashiers) (71%)
4. Customer toilets (70%)
5. Good bike parking possibilities (67%)

The consumer wants supermarkets to extend their range even further. Products and services that the consumer also likes/wants to avail in the supermarket are

- Medicines without a prescription (71%)
- Map and ticket sales (69%)
- Liquor (68%)
- Photo service (64%)
- Office supplies (64%)

There are also annoyances:

- Long wait at checkout (28%)
- Discontinued items (23%)
- Refill during opening hours (22%)
- Sold-out items (21%)
- Sold-out listings (19%)

7.1.1.5 Technological   Technology is constantly changing and, for the most part, improving for the better. However, technological advances and improvements are not intensely relevant for this firm and industry. The extent of the technology used in such a firm is limited to programs, processes, and procedures that are designed to facilitate the online delivery process.

The facilitation of the online delivery firm could occur through advances and improvements in programs used. Programs include those used for taking, processing, and tracking customers' online orders and grocery lists. Improvements in the technology behind those programs could help to reduce the time needed to process a customer's order, thus reducing the time between order and delivery, making delivery times shorter. Newer and more advanced technologies could also help reduce the amount of errors made while processing orders.

Furthermore, a technological look at the processes used within the supermarket sector itself will reveal that the most important programs used are, among other things, programs to keep and track inventory and to maintain a smooth running check-out/purchase and payment system.

The latter technological programs, and thus its advances, are not necessarily directly relevant to this firm. It is, however, indirectly relevant to the firm through its partnerships with various supermarkets. Thus, if, for example, technological advances help to improve a supermarkets, efficiency in inventory turnover and stock-keeping procedures, then these advances and improvements could also be indirectly passed on to the online firm and perhaps even improve its operations as well.

7.1.2 Competition Analysis

Michael Porter's five forces model describes the crucial forces that influence a firm as being *potential entrants, buyers, substitutes, and suppliers*. This section does not discuss the role of substitutes as they are not crucial to this particular industry.

7.1.2.1 Rivalry *Life...to go!*'s competitors (mainly AH) are crucial to the company due to the fact that they are much more experienced with the industry and the market than *Life...to go!* is. Their experience is mainly based on the core business of a physical supermarket itself and its activities, but that experience carries a lot of weight over into the concept of an online delivery service for groceries. Their leadership positioning along with their almost oligopolistic position within the market allows them to have a fairly significant and incredibly crucial amount to say when it comes to new entrants within the market. This makes their bargaining power extremely high and feasible.

7.1.2.2 Suppliers *Life...to go!*'s suppliers and partners can almost be seen as one in the same. This is due to the fact that the online delivery service will be working together with various supermarkets that currently do not offer such a service themselves. As such, *Life...to go!* will in effect be drawing upon the inventories of these supermarkets and using these as the actual physical goods that customers are purchasing online in order for *Life...to go!* to fulfill its service,

making their relationship not only a partnership but also, in broad terms, a supplier–retailer relationship. Due to the importance of these relationships and the fact that they are the backbone of *Life… to go!* makes the firm's partners/suppliers powerful stakeholders of the company. This makes their bargaining power extremely high, almost to the point of crippling.

7.1.2.3 Customers   *Life…to go!* is targeting the entire population (i.e., anyone who, at one point or the other, goes to a supermarket to buy groceries) with a special interest in persons who lead extremely busy lives and cannot find the time in the day to go grocery shopping. Given the nature of *Life…to go!*, customers are crucial to the company as with any firm. If *Life…to go!* fails to sell its *new concept* and attract customers, the company will be doomed. The customers in this company are the foundation of the firm and without them and their support, there would be no service to deliver. This makes their bargaining power extremely high, if not necessary for the survival, transparency, and constant review of the firm.

7.1.2.4 New Arrivals   The industry on a whole, including the large and established players within the market, may not face such defined challenges; however, these are potential and very real challenges that any firm in this industry, whether established and experienced or not, may face. The degree to which a firm may experience such challenges may differ but the core of each challenge remains the same for players within the market, regardless of its size and status.

The only significant difference is that of the supplier/partnership relationship. The main players within the industry do not have such relationships as they serve as their own *partner* in a manner of speaking. The supermarkets serve as retailers to the companies who produce the various products, but in regard to the online venture, they already have everything they need in-house and do not need to look elsewhere. This counts for the entire industry on a whole.

7.1.3 Industry Life Cycle

The industry in which this firm is part of has been around for quite some time; however, it is starting to gain true momentum and recognition only now, thanks, in part, to the invention and wide-spread use of the Internet.

Nevertheless, out of the four stages of the industry life cycle, which are the introduction, growth, maturity, and declining stage, this particular firm (as well as the industry itself) is in the *growth* stage of its life within the industry.

Established firms are now mainly focusing on their brand/image as a differentiation tool in order to attract new customers and to keep existing ones, and prices are starting to decline. The level of competition and the amount of new entrants into the market/industry have also begun to steadily rise causing even more difficulties.

Life...to go! can therefore also be seen as a struggling new entrant of sorts. Although the industry in the Netherlands does not consist of many players, the players that are actually present carry a significant amount of weight and they are well known and already established, making this new endeavor of *Life...to go!* a very risky and ambitious one. The firm will be going head-to-head with a few *big-named* players in what can be seen as a volatile and yet still largely *untapped* market and industry.

7.2 Internal Analysis

Table 7.1 shows a summary of internal analysis based on main functions. *Strengths*

- Firm's products/services; breadth of product line
- Ability to gather needed information about markets
- Market share or submarket shares
- Product/service mix and expansion potential; life cycle of key products; profit/sales balance in product/service
- Effective sales organization; knowledge of customer needs
- Product/service image, reputation, and quality
- Imaginative, efficient, and effective sales promotion and advertising
- Pricing strategy and pricing flexibility
- Ability to raise short-term capital
- Ability to raise long-term capital: debt/equity
- Cost of capital relative to industry and competitors

Table 7.1   Internal Analysis Summary

MARKETING	COMPETITORS	INDUSTRY AVERAGE	STAGE OF THE MARKET
Firm's products/services	AH—large company, Boni—small company and DekaMarkt—small company (indirect, nonthreatening competitor because they offer drive-thru service and not direct delivery).	Basic necessities and household items such as food, beverages, and cleaning products. Products that consumers tend to consume day-to-day and tend to buy frequently; once a week, for example.	The firm will be competing with established competitors who are in their growth stage. The firm will be in partnerships with other established supermarkets and will be using their product lines and customer base combined with its services.
Ability to gather needed information about markets	AH has a high ability as they are one of the largest supermarkets in the Netherlands. Boni and DekaMarkt have fewer resources to apply to market research.	Not available.	High, given the fact that the firm is in partnership with established supermarkets. The firm will have had a few years of experience within the industry and thus the ability level will have risen.
Market share	AH has 33.6% (750 stores), Boni—market share N/A (34 stores), DekaMarkt—market share N/A (86 stores). Market share with regards to their online activity is N/A.	In 2010, the yearly turnover for supermarkets in the Netherlands was €32.14 billion, which amounts to 2.5%.	The firm will have a market share of approximately 20%, due to its partnerships with various supermarkets.
Product/service mix and expansion potential	Information N/A for Boni and DekaMarkt, AH probably has plans of expansion in the future as they are currently only available in certain areas.	N/A, however, the service mix and expansion potential throughout the industry is on average quite high.	Service mix and expansion potential will be high due to partnerships and industry experience. There are plans to expand into other, distinctly different industries.
Effective sales organization/customer needs	The knowledge of customer needs for AH is high and may be a bit less for Boni and DekaMarkt.	Not available.	High due to research, partnerships, and on-the-job experience.

(*Continued*)

Table 7.1 (*Continued*) Internal Analysis Summary

	COMPETITORS	INDUSTRY AVERAGE	STAGE OF THE MARKET
Product/service image	AH is well known with a good reputation and image. DekaMarkt and Boni are not really well known.	N/A, however, there are usually a few firms who develop leadership positions within the industry, and they tend to lead the market into various directions through the use of their image and recognition.	The image and reputation of the firm will be gaining recognition and strength. The firm will be focused on building up its image and brand recognition. The quality will have already been established and will continue to grow stronger.
Sales and promotion advertising	For AH, it is extremely high. For DekaMarkt and Boni, it is minimal and not nationwide.	N/A, however, on average, there tends to be significant effort put into building a firms image and customer base. This requires a significant amount of advertising and promotion.	Advertising efforts will be high on the priorities list. The firm will be engaging in more advertising campaigns in order to continue building its image and to maintain its market share as more competitors will be entering the market.
Pricing strategy and flexibility	For AH, it is high; they engage in discounts and specials and because they are one of the largest supermarkets, their strategy is also quite extensive; AH has a cost leadership strategy. Information for Boni and DekaMarkt is N/A.	N/A, however, it can be assumed that a few firms will be leading the price wars with extensive and complex pricing strategies and due to reliable supplier relationships, prices can be as flexible as they choose; setting the industry average.	The firm's pricing strategy will be positioned competitively against their competitors but will also reflect its differentiation strategy. The firms pricing flexibility will be a balance between negotiations with its partners and the industry average.
FINANCE AND ACCOUNTING			
Ability to raise short-term capital	High because they already have established businesses and are known and recognizable.	N/A, however, this should be fairly easy given a concrete and well thought out business plan.	The firm's ability to raise short-term capital will have gotten better as it gains more brand recognition and its customer base and profits grow.

(*Continued*)

Table 7.1 (*Continued*)   Internal Analysis Summary

	COMPETITORS	INDUSTRY AVERAGE	STAGE OF THE MARKET
Ability to raise long-term capital	High because they already have established businesses and are recognizable.	N/A; this may be more difficult to acquire, however, given that investors may have stricter requirements as it involves more capital.	The firm's ability to raise long-term capital will also have improved; however, it may still be difficult to find willing investors for the long term as the firm might still require a bit more experience.
Cost of capital	N/A, but it should be low given their size and market share.	Not available.	The cost of capital will have leveled off by this time and things should be running somewhat smoother for the firm. The firm will have more experience in reducing costs and managing itself more efficiently.
Leverage position	High for AH given the fact that they are a part of Ahold, moderate for Boni and DekaMarkt as they are smaller players in the industry.	Not available.	The firm's leverage position will have improved due to its partnerships and experience within the industry. Also due to its strong image and growing profits, alternative financial strategies will become easier for the firm.
Cost and barriers to entry	Not available.	The average cost of starting an online firm is approximately €25,000 in the Netherlands. The average and most common barrier to entry are getting sufficient capital.	These costs are no longer relevant due to the fact that the firm is now in its growth stage. Costs associated with this stage are mainly related to advertising, defensive strategies against rising competition level, and differentiation strategies in order to counteract declining prices.

(*Continued*)

Table 7.1 (*Continued*) Internal Analysis Summary

	COMPETITORS	INDUSTRY AVERAGE	STAGE OF THE MARKET
			Nevertheless, costs associated with entering this industry are the costs of setting up a website (approx. €25,000), for buying cars, office rent, and also opportunity costs. However, exact figures are unknown.
Effective cost control	N/A, but it can be assumed that given their size and experience that it would be high for all competitors.	Not available.	This will have leveled off due to growing experience and partnerships.
Financial size	Large for AH, moderate to large for Boni and DekaMarkt.	Not available.	The firm's financial size will have grown due to increasing profits, a growing customer base, partnerships, growing investor interest, and experience.
PRODUCTION/OPERATIONS			
Supplier partnership	Unknown for Boni and DekaMarkt. AH does not necessarily have partnerships; the company usually either takes over (acquisitions) other supermarkets or starts their own new endeavors funded by their own capital.	Not available. However, what is said at *competitors* can also be applied to the *industry average*.	Raw materials are not applicable, but the supplier relationships can be considered as partnerships.

(*Continued*)

Table 7.1 (*Continued*)   Internal Analysis Summary

	COMPETITORS	INDUSTRY AVERAGE	STAGE OF THE MARKET
Equipment	N/A, but it can be assumed that these competitors have a lot of resources available for use and given their level of capital, acquiring equipment at a low cost, with maximum efficiency and that benefits them should not be difficult.	Not available.	The firm has all the equipment necessary for running an efficient business. Acquiring such equipment may still be costly compared to its competitors, but the benefits outweigh the costs. There will be limited equipment, but they allow for maximization of efficiency in delivering the firm's service.
PERSONNEL			
Employees' skill and morale	We assume that they have highly skilled technicians and employees. These employees might work in teams that increases communication and boosts morale.	Not available.	Given that it is an online business, there will be few employees. But as the firm is in the growth stage, there will be more skilled employees hired; and experience will have taught the firm's management how to better boost employee morale.
Labor relations costs	AH might have higher costs compared to Boni and DekaMarkt because they are larger and deliver to more cities and also employ more personnel.	N/A, however, it can be assumed that "regular" employees are paid minimum wage relative to their ages and skilled employees will be paid relative to their qualifications.	These will be relatively low because of few personnel but will (continue to) rise with time and as more employees are hired.

(Continued)

Table 7.1 (*Continued*) Internal Analysis Summary

	COMPETITORS	INDUSTRY AVERAGE	STAGE OF THE MARKET
Ability to level peaks and valleys of employment	High ability to level such peaks and valleys because of a large amount of employees. They can afford to have workers working on call for valleys and are able to send employees home for peaks.	Not available.	The ability of the firm to level highs and lows are still relatively low given that there are a few employees; it is crucial to have all available employees working at all times. This situation should become better, however, as more employees are eventually hired.
ORGANIZATION OF GENERAL MANAGEMENT			
Firm's image and prestige	These competitors—AH in particular—are extremely well known and have already built an image for themselves that involves a certain level of prestige.	N/A, however, it is somewhat obvious that it is centered around a few well-known firms such as AH.	The firm's image is growing and gaining recognition. It will already be known among the "internet generation" and the general public but will not yet be at the level of prestige.
Strategic planning system	N/A, however, it can be assumed that these competitors—AH in particular—has an extensive and complex strategic planning system. This is in order for them to maintain their leadership position and competitive advantage.	Not available.	This is not as extensive as that of AH but it will encompass a strategy for maintaining the firm's position, market share, and partnerships but will also include an offensive and defensive strategy with relation to competitors.

- Leverage position: capacity to utilize alternative financial strategies, such as lease or sale
- Cost of entry and barriers to entry
- Effective cost control; ability to reduce cost
- Financial size
- Raw materials cost and availability; supplier relationships
- Efficiency and cost/benefit of equipment
- Employees' skill and morale
- Labor relations costs compared to industry and competition
- Ability to level peaks and valleys of employment
- Firm's image and prestige
- Strategic planning system

7.3 Competitive Advantages and Success Factors

There are approximately 4300 supermarkets in the Netherlands. Only a very small amount of these supermarkets provide the online service that will directly compete with *Life…to go!*

Life…to go!'s main competitors are AH, Boni, and DekaMarkt because they also offer the online grocery delivery service. However, DekaMarkt cannot be considered as a direct competitor of *Life…to go!* because DekaMarkt's online service only provides online preorder of the customer's groceries, after which the customer is still required to physically go to the supermarket to collect their preordered groceries. The largest competitor is AH, which is a part of the Ahold group. AH reportedly had 824 supermarkets in the Netherlands in 2008 with a visitor's rate (usage rate) of 69%.

AH has a cost leadership position in the Dutch market, and as illustrated by the matrix given earlier, this is the best possible strategy to have as it provides both competitive advantage and scope by having low costs while catering to a broad market. Boni and DekaMarkt can be categorized as having a broad differentiation focus because even though their costs are not extremely high, they are still higher than those of AH, and because they also cater to a broad market.

Furthermore, with regard to AH's and Boni's pricing, Boni delivers orders for €5.95 with a minimum purchase of €50. Interesting to note with Boni though is that they operate in cities in the northwestern of

Holland such as Flevopolder, Zwolle, Apeldoorn, Almere, Lelystad, and Zeewolde, whereas *Life...to go!'s* operations will initially be based in the south of Holland.

With regard to AH's pricing, AH delivers orders starting from €3.95 with a minimum purchase of €70 and with no transportation costs included with a purchase of €100 or more.

The Dutch supermarket sector can be divided into three subsectors consisting of *the primary supermarket sector, the secondary supermarket sector, and the tertiary supermarket sector.* These sectors are defined by the customers' perceived quality level combined with the (per week) patronage rate.

The primary sector can be seen as the customers' first choice when shopping for daily groceries. AH is one of the leaders in this sector, and it had a patronage rate of 36.6% per week in 2011.

The secondary sector can be seen as a *substitute* to the primary sector, as customers usually patronize the supermarkets in this sector in certain situations such as due to proximity and convenience of that supermarket when they are pressed for time. In 2011, Boni joined this sector with a patronage percentage of 0.8% per week. This is an improvement for Boni since in 2010 they were considered a part of the tertiary sector with a substantially lower patronage percentage per week. The tertiary sector can be considered a customer's *last resort* when shopping for groceries and will usually be patronized in the absence of or relatively far distance from/or lack of time to go to primary and/or secondary supermarkets.

7.4 Scenarios and Opportunities

7.4.1 Positive and Negative Scenarios for Industry

It can be predicted that in 3–5 years' time,

- Companies (especially new entrants) within this industry may be experiencing difficulties as their individual stakeholders may not be in tune with each other and thus bringing the company down with them.
- Large, monopolistic players may be able to survive challenges that such an industry is inherent to but the smaller, perhaps newer entrants may find it much more difficult to stay afloat.

- The industry will definitely expand and grow larger due to the fact that people's lives are becoming busier by the day and consumers try to fit as many things into a day as possible at the expense of the smaller chores that they do not count as being of high priority. This will increase the need for a variety of online services that will also attract many other new entrants seeking new opportunities and profits in this industry.

7.4.2 Business Opportunities and Threats

7.4.2.1 Opportunities The information provided throughout this report gives way to the following opportunities for *Life...to go!*

- The company will have a strong entry into the market due to its strategy of creating partnerships with already established supermarkets and turning that into a win-win situation for all parties involved.
- The possibility of retaining a significant market share is large due to the fact that the market is currently inhabited by very few firms, leaving space for new entrants with fresh ideas.
- Entering the market may be made easier due to its partnerships, that is, the firm will immediately have access to a variety of product mix/offering and expansion potential, and the firm will also initially be *riding on the coattails* of its partners, utilizing their well-known images as it gradually builds its own.
- Moreover, the laws regarding opening times mentioned in the external analysis under legislation also provide an opportunity for *Life...to go!* as being an online-based service to be open, in effect, 24 h a day, 7 days a week, and 365 days a year. Of course, delivery will not be done at all hours of the day and night, but this allows consumers to preorder their groceries and to have them delivered the following day, for example. This, once again, proves the effectiveness, efficiency, and value that *Life...to go!'s* customers stand to gain.
- Finally, the points mentioned earlier, in the section of the external analysis regarding the sociocultural aspect, show

gaps in what supermarkets currently offer customers and what customers perceive to still be missing in this service, which translates into what they would like to see throughout the industry as a whole.

These gaps are opportunities for *Life...to go!*, opportunities with great chances of becoming a reality because the company can use such information in its expansion plans by offering some of the products and items that consumers cannot currently get in their preferred supermarkets. Not only is the company already providing convenience, ease of purchase, and efficiency by being an online-based service, but *Life...to go!* can capitalize on this and the supermarkets' flaws by becoming an entirely invaluable one stop shop for consumers.

7.4.2.2 Threats The information provided throughout this report gives way to the following threats of *Life...to go!*:

- The firm is highly inexperienced and unknown.
- Retaining partnerships is an assumption, and there is no guarantee that supermarkets will be willing to partner with *Life...to go!*:
- Barriers to entry will be made significantly more difficult due to semimonopolistic players in the industry.
- The firm will initially be *riding on the coattails* of its partners, utilizing their well-known images as it gradually builds its own; this leaves the firm vulnerable to threats mainly related to its partners. For example, if one of the partners falls on hard times or goes through a very public controversy, this will be reflected on *Life...to go!* as well even though the two may have nothing to do with each other.
- Retaining significant capital may prove difficult due to the fact that *Life...to go!* is highly inexperienced and *green* as they say. And if the potential partners decide/agree to invest within the company, this may signify new and different challenges to the firm such as potentially losing control of its own operations and possibly even losing its identity.
- The firm has minimal to no leveraging position.

7.5 Strategic Objectives, Main Goals, and Main Strategies

7.5.1 Strategic Objective and Main Goals

Life…to go!'s objectives will be *strategic* in nature.

In the coming years, the fight for supermarket customers will not be situated in the shop but on the Internet, and AH has a (huge) lead at the moment. At the moment, AH is currently the only supermarket with a relevant online presence. It can be assumed that from 2016 they will have a market share of more than 50%. The online supermarket in 2016 will be good for a turnover of approximately €700 million, which will ensure that there will be a revolution in this sector. And if online becomes popular and large, then AH will have most of the industry's growth and will be able to hijack turnover away from its competitors.

Life…to go! wants to enter the market when the online supermarket sector is still relatively small (1% market share) and position itself next to the number one supermarket in the Netherlands (within 3–5 years) at the moment, AH. *Life…to go!* believes it can differentiate itself from AH by taking other supermarkets under their wings, and basically partnering with these supermarkets. In this way, *Life…to go!* will become the next best online supermarket (supplier) with a range of multiple supermarkets for consumers to choose from, thereby giving consumers more options of online grocery shopping to choose from (larger variety).

Finally, since it has been predicted that the online supermarket sector will increase in the coming years, *Life…to go!* will have a better chance of entering the market now while the competition level is still very low, and the company can then grow (its market share) and expand over the coming years and position itself as a significant competitor alongside AH. *Life…to go!* wants to partner with some of the largest supermarkets and competitors next to AH, such as Jumbo (second largest supermarket in the Netherlands), Super de Boer, Bas van der Heijden, and Coop. Hereby the supermarkets will not have to open their own individual businesses online and all the resources and financial costs that come along with it. *Life…to go!* will provide them the same opportunities, with fewer risks and the company basically does all the work for them. This is a win-win situation for all parties involved, which will make *Life...to go!* the only online business with various supermarkets to choose from in the Netherlands.

7.5.2 *Main Strategies*

The most appropriate strategies for *Life...to go!* are *market penetration* and *product development*.

Market penetration strategy was chosen because the company will initially have to be aggressive within the market as both the market and the product (in this case, the service) is already known/existent. And as *Life...to go!* cannot modify the product and because the market and industry is a highly competitive one, it may be challenging at first. Therefore, this strategy calls for much determination and perseverance, and with hard work, the goals and objectives will be met.

This strategy was chosen as a precautionary method with the future in mind. After establishing its presence and making a name for itself, *Life...to go!* will need to seek new ways of surviving, staying fresh, and keeping its customers as the *penetration* strategy might no longer be viable, hence the need for a product development strategy or, in this case, more like a *service* development strategy. The word *service* is used because the company has no control over the development of the tangible products (i.e., groceries) handled and delivered by them. This strategy is necessary because it will ensure future survival and profitability, not to mention a competitive edge over its competitors. It will be crucial for the company to develop new or modified ways of delivering its service while still granting a high customer satisfaction level. Because of these reasons, it is wise for the company to have such a strategy in mind now and to begin working on the essentials of such a strategy early in the game before it is too late in order to be prepared for whatever may come.

8

NATURAL FOOD*

Vision

To be the world's premier natural food company, offering natural products comprising superior tasting and highest quality to individuals having gusto and opting for natural life.

Mission

Providing individuals (opting for natural life and gusto) superior tasting and highest-quality natural food products by unique, innovative, and clean production process that improves the quality of individuals' life, provides employees meaningful work and maximum rate of return to investors, and contributes sustainability in ecologic life.

Basic Policies

Natural Food offers treasures of Anatolia from the Aegean region of Turkey. The olive tree and its oil are age-old symbols of health. Natural Food brings customers the superior tasting in natural nutrition with certified products in the light of values as responsibility, honesty, accuracy, and transparency:

- Long-term profitability is fundamental to accomplish our business goals and sustainable growth. It supplies the essential corporate resources for continual investment that is required to produce and serve natural foods to meet customer needs and to contribute sustainability in ecologic life.
- Compete ethically and fairly according to the framework of applicable competition laws.

---

* This case study was contributed by Pınar Senoğlu.

- Insist on transparency, integrity, and honesty in all aspects of our business and expect the same in our relationships with all those that we do business.
- Comply with all applicable laws and regulations of the countries in which we operate.
- Insist on realizing production and after-sale services by considering health, safety, and environment.
- Contribute local production and work with others to enhance the benefits to local communities, and to mitigate any negative impacts from our activities.

8.1 Environmental Analysis

8.1.1 Macroeconomic Analysis

8.1.1.1 Demographic   Indicators show that the population is increasing. This situation will affect businesses positively in terms of work force and customers who search for healthy nutrition.

Education level: For businesses that target customers who search for high-quality taste and healthy nutrition, an increase in education level will positively affect them.

8.1.1.2 Judicial–Political   *Incentives*: The olive oil sector and exporting are supported by the government.

Green laws: Today, green production and products have important roles in different industries.

Political stability: Recent developments in Turkey show that political stability has a significant role for businesses. Therefore, businesses will be negatively affected from the current political climate.

8.1.1.3 Economic   *Distribution of income*: Inequality in distribution of income will continue, which will limit targeted customers.

Foreign exchange policy: The general trend of the government is to support exporting and foreign investment.

Degree of international trade: Due to globalization, restrictions, trade barriers, and tariffs will be more flexible, which will have a direct impact on businesses.

8.1.1.4 Sociocultural Trends show that a healthier lifestyle has become an important issue.

8.1.1.5 Natural Environment Indicators show that due to climate changes, water shortages will occur, which will have a negative impact on our industry. Therefore, there is a need to develop a new irrigation system for olive trees.

8.1.1.6 Technological In the light of organic production perspective, there is a need to systematize R&D activities for improving production quality and preventing natural production volatility of olive trees.

8.1.2 Competition Analysis

The global olive oil market is one of the fastest growing segments of the global food industry, showing significant growth year after year. Olive oil is the main component of the Mediterranean diet, the health properties of which makes olive oil a food product with a promising future.

The global olive oil market grew by 3% between 2008 and 2012, but this growth rate varied widely across different markets. Traditional consumer countries in the North Mediterranean, that is, Italy, Spain, and Greece, have the highest per capita consumption (more than 12 kg per person) but are characterized as a very mature and stagnating market. In contrast, developed markets offer significant potential in terms of both value (at present, they account for 41% of the global market) and growth, with levels projected to continue at around 4% for at least the next 5 years.

Emerging markets hold the greatest potential for the olive oil industry, posting an impressive 13% growth rate over the last 5 years. Brazil and China are the two most important countries in terms of volume and producers. China imported 45,000 tons of olive oil in 2012 and became a crucial market for producers. Several major state-owned enterprises (SOE) have been increasing their imports of bulk olive oil from southern Europe.

Private label (PL) products and A-brands represent the primary growth opportunities in developed countries. In the United Kingdom, the most developed food retailer market, the PL share in olive oil accounts for almost 5%, while it accounts for 25% in the United States and 20% in the most fragmented Italian market. The latter two markets and several other northern European markets provide other interesting growth opportunities.

There are factors that will restrict the industry's ability to realize its ambitions in emerging markets. First, there is a need for all players to strengthen their strategic sourcing options. Second, a generic marketing campaign is required in emerging markets to educate consumers about the benefits and versatility of olive oil.

Spain is the largest producer and exporter of olive oil in the world followed by Italy, while the United States is the third largest consumer of olive oil after Spain and Italy. The consumption pattern of olive oil in the BRIC countries has shown tremendous growth. It is expected that in the near future India and China will be on the list of largest consumers of olive oil as people have started recognizing the health benefits of olive oil and have accepted it as cooking oil.

As the production of olive oil is limited to some specific geography, pricing of olive oil sees major fluctuations when production or cultivation gets affected.

Turkey's olive oil exports have dramatically increased to over 45,000 tons, with a 446% rise in the last 5 months compared to the same period a year earlier. The rise is due to a considerable fall in the harvest of Spain, the world's largest oil producer, according to a sector report.

Turkey's olive oil exports, which had been halted considerably since the 2005–2006 season, started to recover last year. While exports increased to 20,000 tons in the 2011–2012 seasons, from 12,000 tons in the previous period, income from exports reached $65 million, with a 33% increase.

The new season showed more than 400% increases in both the amount of exports and the value. As the exports reached 45,524 tons with a 446% increase between November 2012 and March 2013, the export value reached $143 million with a 406% increase. The exports in March soared by 626% on a year-on-year basis.

The report revealed that a 60% loss in Spain's olive oil production because of lack of rain had boosted Turkey's exports. The 95,000 tons of olive oil production hike in Italy and Greece could not fill the gap in the market, and the European Union's removal of the customs duty on Turkey's olive oil exports also helped Turkey. Despite the recent fall, Spain still remains the largest olive oil producer in the world, followed by Italy, Greece, Tunisia, and Turkey. Figures 8.1 and 8.2 show the competitive forces status.

8.2 Internal Analysis

Table 8.1 shows the strengths and weaknesses of the firm based on functional approach.

8.3 Competitive Advantages and Success Factors

Table 8.2 is a comparison of the firm with main competitor and industry average that ends up with competitive advantages and success factors of the firm, which are shown in Table 8.3.

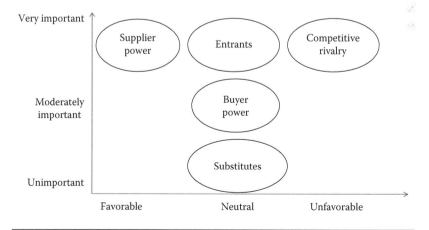

Figure 8.1 Competitive forces.

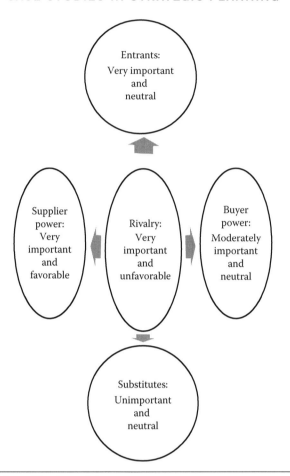

Figure 8.2   Competitive forces status.

8.4 Scenarios and Opportunities

8.4.1 Positive and Negative Scenarios for Industry

Positive scenarios

- Expectations on the change in lifestyles will continue and healthier lifestyles have become more of an issue. Therefore, educational level, awareness, and demand of organic and natural products will increase.
- People who can afford high prices and superior tasting olive oil will increase.
- Due to the high potentials of olive oil exporting, incentives and laws against monopolization will continue. Turkey has

Table 8.1 Functional Approach Worksheet

	FACTORS	STRENGTHS/ WEAKNESSES
Marketing	Firm's products/services; breadth of product line	−
	Concentration of sales in a few products or to a few customers	−
	Ability to gather needed information about markets	+
	Market share or submarket shares	−
	Product/service mix and expansion potential	+
	Channels of distribution: number, coverage, and control	−
	Effective sales organization	−
	Product/service image, reputation, and quality	−
	Imaginative, efficient, and effective sales promotion and advertising	+
	Pricing strategy and pricing flexibility	−
	Procedures for digesting market feedback and developing new products, services, or markets	+
	After-sale service and follow-up	+
	Goodwill/brand loyalty	−
Finance and accounting	Ability to raise short-term capital	+
	Ability to raise long-term capital: debt/equity	−
	Corporate-level resources	−
	Cost of capital relative to industry and competitors	+
	Tax considerations	−
	Relations with owners, investors, and stockholders	−
	Leverage positions	+
	Cost of entry and barriers to entry	+
	Price-to-earnings ratio	−
	Working capital; flexibility of capital structure	−
	Effective cost control, ability to reduce costs	−
	Financial size	−
	Efficient and effective accounting system for cost, budget, and profit planning	+
Production/ operations/ technical	Raw materials cost and availability	+
	Inventory control systems; inventory turnover	+
	Location of facilities; layout and utilization of facilities	+
	Economies of scale	−
	Technical efficiency of facilities and utilization of capacity	+
	Effective use of subcontracting	+
	Degree of vertical integration, value added, and profit margin	−
	Efficiency and cost/benefit of equipment	+
	Effective operation control procedures	+

(*Continued*)

Table 8.1 (*Continued*)   Functional Approach Worksheet

	FACTORS	STRENGTHS/ WEAKNESSES
	Cost and technological competencies relative to industry and competitors	+
	Research and development/technology/innovation	+
	Patents, trademarks, and similar legal protection	+
Personnel	Management personnel	+
	Employees' skill and morale	+
	Labor relations cost compared to industry and competition	−
	Efficient and effective personnel policies	+
	Effective use of incentives to motivate performance	+
	Ability to level peaks and valleys of employment	+
	Employee turnover and absenteeism	−
	Specialized skills	+
	Experience	+
Organization/ general management	Organizational structure	+
	Firm's image and prestige	−
	Firm's record for achieving objectives	−
	Organization of communication system	+
	Overall organizational control system	+
	Organizational climate, culture	+
	Use of systematic procedures and techniques in decision making	+
	Top-management skill, capacities, and interest	+
	Strategic planning system	+
	Intraorganizational synergy	+

approximately 5% market share in world olive oil production. The statistics show that the demand for olive oil in emerging markets has grown at a rate of over 13% since 2007, and such double-digit growth is expected to continue at least for the next 5 years. Accordingly, by considering the increasing trend of olive oil demand, Turkey has the potential to increase its market share as well.

Negative scenarios

- Rich soil shortages may cause negative impacts on the additional supply of olive trees and quality of products. In addition, climate changes and water shortages may negatively affect production.

Table 8.2 Comparison Table

	FACTORS	NATURAL	MAIN COMP.	INDUSTRY
Marketing	Firm's products/services; breadth of product line	−	−	−
	Concentration of sales in a few products or to a few customers	−	−	−
	Ability to gather needed information about markets	+	+	−
	Market share or submarket shares	−	−	−
	Product/service mix and expansion potential	+	+	−
	Channels of distribution: number, coverage, and control	−	−	−
	Effective sales organization	−	−	−
	Product/service image, reputation, and quality	−	+	−
	Imaginative, efficient, and effective sales promotion and advertising	+	−	−
	Pricing strategy and pricing flexibility	−	−	+
	Procedures for digesting market feedback and developing new products, services, or markets	+	+	−
	After-sale service and follow-up	+	−	−
	Goodwill/brand loyalty	−	−	−
Finance and accounting	Ability to raise short-term capital	+	+	+
	Ability to raise long-term capital: debt/equity	−	+	−
	Corporate-level resources	−	−	−
	Cost of capital relative to industry and competitors	+	+	−
	Tax considerations	−	−	−
	Relations with owners, investors, and stockholders	−	−	−
	Leverage positions	+	+	−
	Cost of entry and barriers to entry	+	+	−
	Price-to-earnings ratio	−	+	
	Working capital; flexibility of capital structure	−	+	−
	Effective cost control, ability to reduce costs	−	+	−
	Financial size	−	−	−

(*Continued*)

Table 8.2 (*Continued*) Comparison Table

	FACTORS	NATURAL	MAIN COMP.	INDUSTRY
	Efficient and effective accounting system for cost, budget, and profit planning	+	−	−
Production/ technical	Raw materials cost and availability	+	+	+
	Inventory control systems; inventory turnover	+	−	−
	Location of facilities; layout and utilization	+	+	+
	Economies of scale	−	−	−
	Technical efficiency of facilities and utilization of capacity	+	−	−
	Effective use of subcontracting	+	+	+
	Degree of vertical integration, value added, and profit margin	−	−	−
	Efficiency and cost/benefit of equipment	+	−	−
	Effective operation control procedures	+	−	−
	Cost and technological competencies relative to industry and competitors	+	−	−
	Research and development/ technology/innovation	+	−	−
	Patents, trademarks, and similar	+	−	−
Personnel	Management personnel	+	+	−
	Employees' skill and morale	+	−	−
	Labor relations cost compared to industry and competition	−	+	+
	Efficient and effective personnel policies	+	−	−
	Effective use of incentives to motivate performance	+	−	−
	Ability to level peaks and valleys of employment	+	−	−
	Employee turnover and absenteeism	−	+	−
	Specialized skills	+	−	
	Experience	+	+	+
Organization of general management	Organizational structure	+	−	−
	Firm's image and prestige	−	+	−
	Firm's record for achieving objectives	−	+	−

(*Continued*)

Table 8.2 (*Continued*)   Comparison Table

FACTORS	NATURAL	MAIN COMP.	INDUSTRY
Organization of communication system	+	–	–
Overall organizational control system	+	–	–
Organizational climate, culture	+	+	–
Use of systematic procedures and techniques	+	–	–
Top-management skill, capacities, and interest	+	+	–
Strategic planning system	+	–	–
Intraorganizational synergy	+	+	–

- Due to the current negative political and economic conditions, the businesses may become more volatile.

8.4.2 Business Opportunity

People who can afford high prices and superior tasting and highest-quality olive oil will increase, and this niche market will be met by strong management skills, specialized product and service performances, and effective distribution channels. Figure 8.3 shows the Big Bang and Milky Way as business opportunities.

8.5 Main Goals and Main Strategies

8.5.1 Main Goals

- Providing services to specific and high-level customers with highest-quality products
- Producing highest-quality natural olive oil by unique and innovative production processes
- Contributing sustainability in ecologic life via clean production processes
- Satisfying higher needs of people who search for gusto
- Being an exporter

Table 8.3 Competitive Advantages and Success Factors

	FACTORS	COMPETITIVE ADVANTAGES	SUCCESS FACTORS
Organization of general management	1. Flexible and horizontal relations facilitate decision making		
	2. Participatory and sharing management		
	3. Broad investment vision		
	4. Prestigious company name		
	5. Experienced management staff undertaking responsibilities		
	6. Strategic planning	+	
Personnel	1. Competent, experienced, and responsible staff		+
	2. Qualified and young labor force	+	
	3. Specialized staff	+	
Production and technical	1. Ease of raw material supply		+
	2. Good supplier relations		
	3. Registered trademarks	+	
	4. Effective use of subcontractors		+
	5. Cost and technological competencies relative to industry and competitors	+	
	6. Production control procedures	+	
	7. Effective quality control	+	
	8. Vertical integration		
	9. Technical team competence	+	
	10. Product development capacity	+	
	11. Development potential of products	+	
Marketing	1. Product diversity		
	2. Market leader		
	3. Pre-sales application service	+	
	4. Qualification and competence in distribution channels		
	5. Quality and branded products		
	6. Technical support department		
	7. Strong references		
Finance and accounting	1. Automation and integration through system investments, resulting in effective accounting, costing, and budgeting	+	
	2. Effective cost control		
	3. High credibility		

(Continued)

Table 8.3 (*Continued*)   Competitive Advantages and Success Factors

FACTORS	COMPETITIVE ADVANTAGES	SUCCESS FACTORS
4. Positive communication with shareholders, strong shareholder		
5. High equity profitability		
6. High working capital ratio		
7. High profit margin	+	

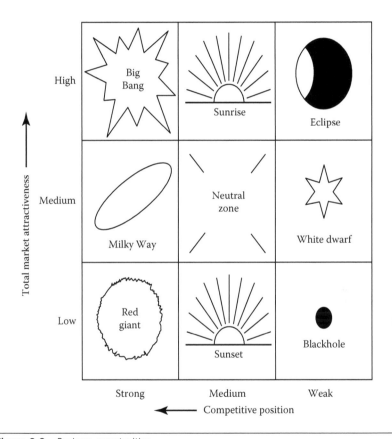

Figure 8.3   Business opportunities.

- Providing employees meaningful working life
- Working with best employees
- Improving employees' self-esteem and training them to get maximum productivity
- Improving R&D activities

Competitive Advantage

	Low Cost	Differentiation
Broad	*1. Cost leadership*	*2. Differentiation*
Narrow	*3a. Cost focus*	*3b. Differentiation focus*

Scope

Figure 8.4 Generic competitive strategies.

Product / Market	Present	New
Present	*Market penetration*	*Product development*
New	*Market development*	*Diversification*

Figure 8.5 Components of strategy.

8.5.2 Main Strategies

Providing high-priced products to high-level consumers who search for gusto and natural olive oil. Figure 8.4 shows the differentiation focusing as a strategy.

Changing consumption styles of high-level customers who search for gusto by new product and service concepts. Figure 8.5 shows the product development as a strategy.

9

9
SPEEDY*

Mission

Speedy provides the most convenient and innovative technology for easy, quick, and painless note taking to business professionals and students.

9.1 Environmental Analysis

9.1.1 Macroeconomic Analysis

9.1.1.1 Demographic 15–64-year-old people in Turkey (who are at working ages) constitute 67.2% of the total population, which is in our target segment. Furthermore, in Turkey, there are 24,631,831 students who take notes every day. Table 9.1 shows the education distribution in Turkey.

Employment: Tables 9.2 and 9.3 show labor force statuses in Turkey.

Left-handed group: In 1998, a study suggested that approximately 7%–10% of the adult population was left-handed, and that left-handedness is more common in males than females. Among other difficulties, writing is a very important problem for that group of people and this difficulty forces them to write by a very inconvenient writing style.

9.1.1.2 Judicial–Political Writing for the World Bank's *Governance Matters* in 2009, authors Kaufmann, Kraay, and Mastruzzi assign Turkey a score of −0.73 for the factor *Political Stability and Absence of Violence/Terrorism* in the report's governance indicators for 1996–2008. These indicators are normally distributed around a mean of zero. Higher scores signify less violence and greater political stability in a society.

---

* This case study was contributed by Önder Onaran, Aylin Pamuk, and Tuğçe Uzun.

Table 9.1   Education Distribution in Turkey

	2008/09	2009/10	% GROWTH	2010/11	% GROWTH
General total	22,155,563	23,199,865	4.7	24,631,831	62
Total of formal education	15,351,849	16,137,436	5.1	16,845,528	4.4
Pre-primary	804,765	980,654	21.9	1,115,818	13.8
Primary	10,709,920	10,916,643	1.9	10,981,100	0.6
Secondary	3,837,164	4,240,139	10.5	4,748,610	12.0
Nonformal education	6,803,714	7,062,429	3.8	7,786,303	10.2

Table 9.2   Labor Force Status of "15–24 Age Group" by Years

	UNEMPLOYMENT RATE%	LABOR FORCE PARTICIPATION RATE%	EMPLOYMENT RATE%
2008	20.5	38.1	30.3
2009	25.3	38.7	28.9
2010	21.7	38.3	30.0
(First 4 month's average) 2011	20.0	37.4	29.9

Table 9.3   Labor Force Status by Noninstitutional Population, Years (15+ Ages)

	UNEMPLOYMENT RATE%	LABOR FORCE PARTICIPATION RATE%	EMPLOYMENT RATE%
2008	11.0	46.9	41.7
2009	14.0	47.9	41.2
2010	11.9	48.8	43.0
(First 4 month's average) 2011	11.0	48.9	43.5

The U.S. Department of State's 2010 background note on Turkey notes that, following a military coup in 1980, Turkey drafted a constitution (enacted in 1982) that established a democratic, secular, parliamentary form of government. Vagueness in the law regarding presidential power means that a president's ultimate influence is dependent upon personality and persuasiveness. Executive power is shared between the president and the prime minister, the latter of whom serves as the leader of the council of ministers. Beginning in 2007, the presidential term was reduced by constitutional amendment from 7 to 5 years, with a two-term maximum. The president is elected by direct popular vote.

Parliament members are elected according to *party-list proportional representation*, which is based on minimum national and district voting percentages. Passage of a parliamentary vote on which a popular referendum has been held requires a 60% vote (330 of the 550 members); otherwise, a two-thirds majority is required.

The judiciary is nominally independent, but the U.S. Department of Commerce's 2010 country commercial guide notes that there are perceptions that the judicial system is subject to political interference. The DoS adds that Turkey has a Constitutional Court, a Supreme Court of Appeals, a Council of State, a Court of Accounts, and a Military Court of Appeals. Supervision of the judiciary is carried out by the presidentially appointed High Council of Judges.

To sum up, the stable political environment in Turkey will be advantageous in establishing a new business in Turkey.

9.1.1.3 Economic Turkey's economy is increasingly driven by its industry and service sectors, although its traditional agriculture sector still accounts for about 30% of employment. An aggressive privatization program has reduced state involvement in basic industry, banking, transport, and communication, and an emerging cadre of middle-class entrepreneurs is adding dynamism to the economy.

Turkey's traditional textiles and clothing sectors still account for one-third of industrial employment, despite the stiff competition in international markets that resulted from the end of the global quota system.

Other sectors, notably the automotive, construction, and electronics industries, are rising in importance and have surpassed textiles within Turkey's export mix.

Oil began to flow through the Baku-Tbilisi-Ceyhan pipeline in May 2006, marking a major milestone that will bring up to one million barrels per day from the Caspian to the market. Several gas pipelines also are being planned to help move Central Asian gas to Europe via Turkey, which will help address Turkey's dependence on energy imports over the long term.

After Turkey experienced a severe financial crisis in 2001, Ankara adopted financial and fiscal reforms as part of an IMF program. The reforms strengthened the country's economic fundamentals and ushered in an era of strong growth, averaging more than 6% annually until 2008, when global economic conditions and tighter fiscal policy caused GDP to contract in 2009; reduced inflation to 6.3%, a 34-year low; and cut the public sector debt-to-GPD ratio below 50%. Turkey's well-regulated financial markets and banking system weathered the global financial crisis and GDP rebounded strongly to 7.3% in 2010, as exports returned to normal levels following the recession. The economy, however, continues to be burdened by a high current account deficit and remains dependent on often volatile, short-term investment to finance its trade deficit. The stock value of FDI stood at $174 billion during the end of 2010, but inflows have slowed, in the light of continuing economic turmoil in Europe, the source of Turkey's FDI.

Further economic and judicial reforms and prospective EU membership are expected to boost Turkey's attractiveness to foreign investors. However, Turkey's relatively high current account deficit, uncertainty related to policymaking, and fiscal imbalances leave the economy vulnerable to destabilizing shifts in investor confidence.

9.1.2 Competition Analysis

9.1.2.1 Rivalry   Pilot: Despite high customer awareness, Pilot has been losing blood since 2000 against Speedy. The distributor of Pilot is a strong company and offers a variety of brands to the market. They mostly focused their attention on liquid ink roller ball category, and they do not have a similar or equivalent product yet in the Turkish market.

However, they introduced an equivalent product, Acroball, in other markets. Pilot positions this pen as *a new generation of ink for out-of-the-ordinary writing flow and smoothness.*

Pentel: Pentel is a Japanese competitor that offers very important products to the market. BK77 is very popular in the market and gained a very good position. Despite its simple design, its smoothness is the most distinctive feature of the product.

Another distinctive product of Pentel is Hyper G, which was introduced in September 2008. As a gel ink roller ball pen, Hyper G offers only four colors and only a retractable version is available. In Turkey, consumers prefer with cap versions mostly. Pentel's position statement is: *Hyper G guarantees an ultra-smooth writing experience every time and boasts archival quality ink to protect important documents against fraud.*

Papermate: Papermate is a rival brand in the United States, but they are not a well-known brand in Turkey. In the last year, Sanford, the owner of the Papermate and Rotring brand, acquired the Turkish distributor as a forward integration policy. They introduced Flexigrip in 2008, and their motto is *Probably the smoothness pen in the world.* Despite the design disadvantage, Flexigrip's core offerings are very similar and the first results seem above the expectation of other market players.

Schneider: Schneider is a famous German brand in Turkey, and they offer a variety of goods in Turkey. They offer Glider in 2008 to the market, and they positioned this gel ink pen as a superior smooth pen. Their motto *High speed glider from Schneider* emphasized that they are a competitor of Speedy in the sense of smooth feature.

Zebra: Zebra is another Japanese pen manufacturer. They introduced emulsion ink in 2011. Their strategy is very similar to the other brands; they also would like to give a name to hybrid ink technology. They also claimed that they invented this ink in order to get the advantages of oil-based ink and water-based ink.

As can be seen in Table 9.4, most of the well-known brands have some activities to rejuvenate their products. They introduce new phenomenon to the industry. But these brands are not able to create a distinctive difference in the market because of the following:

- Low involvement of the customers create a distinctive problem for these brands.
- Not having a distinctive image.
- Their wide range of products harms the awareness of the consumers.
- They target broad segment and it prevents them to allocate their resources effectively.

9.1.2.2 Customers The writing instruments industry offers lots of new products that can be categorized (shown in Figure 9.1) as follows:

- *Free ink roller ball pen*: The ink is in liquid phase and a rolling ball transmits the ink onto the paper fibers. The production of free ink roller ball pens requires high tech because it is more likely to leak in case of any possible production defect.

Table 9.4 Features of Well-Known Brands

PRODUCT	FEATURES
Pentel Hyper G	Gel roller ball has a fade-resistant and waterproof archival-quality ink. The ink is quick drying and highly resistant to water, acetone, bleach, and acid. Contoured rubber grip and distinctive diamond-cut inner barrel decoration. Chromed nose with unusual accent.
Pentel BK77	Superior-quality basic ball point. Slim line crystal-clear barrel and polished chrome nose stand out from the cheapie alternatives, while the ink is delivered smoothly and cleanly until the last drop. The pen tip is even cleaned each time the cap is replaced. 0.7 mm nib writes a 0.35 mm line. Available in black, blue, red, green, violet, or pink ink. Uses BKL7 refill.
Schneider Slider	ViscoGlide technology. The new hybrid ink plus *Direct2Point* tip guarantees instant ink flow and a smooth writing experience. Capped design with a nonslip grip zone.xtra-Broad point writes approx. 0.7 mm line. Fast drying ink available in black, blue, red, green, orange, purple/violet, pink, light blue, or light green. Black ink is waterproof.
Papermate FlexiGlide	Soft grip that extends along the length of the barrel. Lubriglide and Ink System provide smooth writing. Also available in retractable and with cap model. Refillable. Available in blue, black, red, and purple.
Zebra Surari	Zebra introduced its brand new hybrid ink *Emulsion Ink* in this product. Nine colors for 0.7 mm tip size and three color option for 1.0 mm tip size.

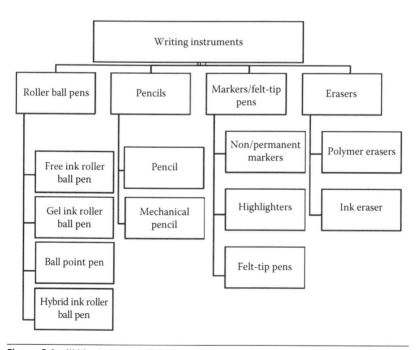

Figure 9.1 Writing instruments industry product category.

- *Gel ink roller ball pen*: The ink is in gel phase. By the help of the rolling ball, the viscosity of gelled ink turns to liquid, so that the ball can transmit the ink onto the paper.
- *Ball point pen*: It is the oldest form of roller ball pens. The oil-based ink requires much more pressure than other types of pens. The most common and commoditized pen types are widely used as a promotion material.
- *Pencil*: Writing instruments that consist of a thin rod of graphite and a cylindrical barrel. Nowadays, the consumption patterns shifted to mechanical pencils where the graphite lead is pushed out of the pen by a mechanical system.
- *Markers*: A marker pen, marking pen, felt-tip pen, or marker, is a pen that has its own ink source, and usually has a tip made of a porous material, such as felt or nylon. The manufacturers produce a lot of markers for different purposes, for example, window marker, whiteboard marker, highlighter, and textile marker. Despite the old technology it involves, some felt-tip pens are very popular like Point 88 of Stabilo.

The estimations show that the size of the worldwide writing instruments market is $18 billion in 2009. The global crisis squeezed the profits of some of the biggest office products and stationery industry's brands and forced some of the major markets to get smaller, especially in Western Europe and the United States.

The developing economies of the Middle and Far East, much of Asia Pacific, Africa, and South America still keep their healthy growth rates.

Although South America and Asia Pacific regions are not protected from economic troubles, market growth has been stimulated by the rising demand for quality writing instruments and population increase.

Chinese manufacturers still market to the low/mid level of consumers, but it is certain that brightly colored promotional pens, novelty-shaped highlighters and models with flashing LEDs, or retractable paper rolls continue to gain popularity.

Despite the general perception in the global market, the quality of Chinese writing instruments is very low. However, the quality and the range of products are improving every year. Chinese manufacturers tend to focus on novel digital features, ergonomic barrel shapes, environmentally friendly designs such as large-capacity highlighters, markers with reusable ink containers, and pens featuring recycled newspaper barrels. In the recent years, they do not follow the leaders, they innovate their own products.

In the Turkish writing instruments market, we may see a lot of different brands, some of them are Turkish and some international.

The most distinctive problem in the market is that the sizes of the players are relatively small. The number of retail points are approximately 35,000 throughout Turkey and 10,000 of them are located in Istanbul.

It should be noted that the writing instruments sector is an export-based sector and most of the well-known brands are international brands. Some of the international firms have subsidiary establishment in Turkey, and some of them have appointed a distributor in Turkey. However, the distribution system is very concrete for most of the distributors and almost all of them distribute their goods in the same manner.

The most vital issue that we have to take into consideration in understanding the distribution system is that most of the retailers are not professional people but small-scale retailers. The distribution system in the writing instruments industry is shown in Figure 9.2.

Compared with developed economies like the United States, the most important drawback of the Turkish market is the uneducated retailers who have an obvious lack of expertise about stationery. For example,

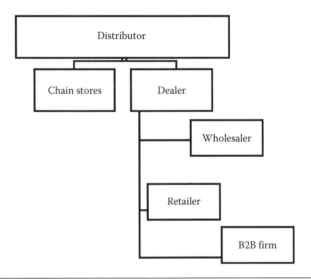

Figure 9.2   Distribution system in the writing instruments industry.

huge stationery retails like Staples, Office Max, or Office Depot are able to run their business in a professional way, and they have expertise about the products and also the retailing of stationery goods. In such cases, the value chain can be assessed much more easily and the costs and price fluctuations can be controlled without suffering the pipeline effect.

We can classify Turkish stationery stores as specialized retail stores, a single unit of retail that carries a specific line of goods and specialized in it. Like other specialty stores such as drug, haberdashery, and hardware stores, the stationery stores focus on stationery and related materials and services.

Another disadvantage of the Turkish stationery sector is the pipeline effect. The most critical issue in the distribution ship design is controlling the risk and finding the most economical and effective functions. Sometimes, the competitive environment and established system constrains the distributors in their selection, as in the Turkish stationery market. Sometimes, the established market conditions make it impossible to work without a middleman. Despite the current situation, the experts can easily forecast that the middleman is disappearing in the modern business world because of the ease with which companies can communicate with and inform consumers about their products.

Despite the fact that distribution channels are modern in developed countries, the Turkish stationery market consists of traditional distribution channels.

The branded writing instruments were distributed according to the chart given earlier. As mentioned earlier, approximately 35,000 companies (retail shops or B2B companies) are operating in this sector, and such a high number of sales points make the distribution system complicated.

Most of the international brands focus on the developing markets to enlarge their businesses. With the help of the young generation, Turkey is definitely one of the most prospective markets. Despite the lack of official data, the approximate size of the writing instruments sector is 200 million USD, whereas the Turkish stationery market is estimated to reach more than 1 billion euro.

The size of the market is still growing because of the young generation of Turkish population, which is around 20 million.

The chain stores are very interested in stationery products because they perceive the stationery sector as an additional revenue source, and they are trying to create a competitive advantage against the competitors.

9.1.3 Industry Life Cycle

There is a debate in branding circles as to whether or not a brand can have a *life cycle* of its own, or whether its peaks and troughs are just a symptom of managing the brand elements, which are its logo, personality, positioning, etc.

In a product life cycle, the peaks and troughs can come in a quicker timeframe, making the cycle more obvious. A brand can have a rise, and then fall out of favor, to be superseded by a new and improved brand. The fact that the branding process takes many years affects the universal acceptance of the existence of a brand life cycle. Without careful management, brands can follow the general pattern of a product life cycle: moving through introduction, growth, maturity, and decline stages in a relatively rapid fashion.

For multiple products, the marketer's task is more complex as he or she needs to map the various life stages of each of the products to stagger and phase them across the product universe in order that each product life cycle is fully optimized for cash generation across the business horizon.

Product rejuvenation ideas could be generated from the perspective of enhancing or changing the product features, adding new usages for the product, enhancing the product manufacturing process, product packaging technological innovation, creative and unique channel delivery process, etc.

We have to create a difference through innovative solutions. Our aim shall be injection of new life to writing instruments.

9.2 Internal Analysis

As a new company, the following internal analysis is conducted:

9.2.1 Marketing

- Our product will fulfill the need of note taking at any time and our product will be easy to access for the consumers.
- It requires an extended product line for a niche segment, which we will be able to accomplish in a short period of time.
- We will decide the portfolio to allow the consumers to be aware of our brand and to position our brand in their mind easily.

- Unlike most of the other writing instruments brands, we will just focus on the *note taking* phenomenon, not on the whole writing instruments segment.
- The products' expansion potential is limited.
- Channels of distribution are kept by the competitors; and as a new brand, we have to fight for a place in the distribution channel.
- Due to the former proficiency, one of our top managers has a deep knowledge about the market and industry.
- We do not have product image and reputation. But we do not have negative image either.
- To create brand awareness, we shall focus on the communication of our brand; however, the sales and distribution promotions will come at the first place. So, we will postpone consumer communication activities for a while.
- Because of start-up costs, we will not be able to have a flexible pricing policy.
- Unfortunately, we do not have enough data to analyze the market.

9.2.2 Production/Operations

- We will outsource the production side of our business to an international writing instruments producer. So it will help us focus on the marketing side of our business.
- Raw materials are very easy to access and the costs are at mid level.
- Because we outsource the production and our job is just stocking a few SKU, a basic control system will be enough at the initial step.
- Location of the production will be in China/Taiwan, so it may cause a time delay in the distribution of the goods.
- Because we will focus on a niche segment and be a new brand whose sales are low, we cannot use the benefits of economies of scale.
- Vertical integration is not possible for now.
- We have technological competency as a result of our state-of-the-art ink formula.
- Research and technology investments will be at minimum in the introduction stage.
- Our patented ink technology is our key asset.

9.2.3 Personnel

- We will employ four new business and administration graduates in the sales department.
- Our salary strategy will be based on performance.
- Our relations with the employees will be much more involved and the management and employees will work as a team.
- We will use incentives to motivate the performance.
- Experience of the personnel will not be enough to compete in the market.
- In order to increase our profitability and decrease costs, we are planning to have a boutique company and a wider hierarchical structure to keep us proactive.

9.2.4 Organization of General Management

- Our company will follow an entrepreneurial management style. Three partners are the head of the following departments: sales, marketing, and finance.
- A wider hierarchical structure will help us to work proactively and react in a short period of time.
- Although the firm does not have a record for achieving objectives, the management team has positive records for achieving objectives.
- As a boutique company, we will have an effective control system because of our size.
- The management has enough skill to start-up and run the company.

9.2.5 Business Strengths and Weaknesses

Strengths

- Unlike most of the other writing instruments brands, we will just focus on the *note taking* phenomenon, not on the whole writing instruments segment.
- Due to the former proficiency, one of our top managers has a deep knowledge about the market and industry.
- Outsourcing production will help us focus on the marketing side of our business.

- Because we outsource the production and our job is just stocking a few SKU, a basic control system will be enough at the initial step.
- We have technological competency as a result of our state-of-the-art ink formula.
- Our company will follow an entrepreneurial management style. Three partners are the head of the following departments: sales, marketing, and finance.
- In order to increase our profitability and decrease costs, we are planning to have a boutique company and a wider hierarchical structure to keep us proactive.
- The management has enough skill to start-up and run the company.

Weaknesses

- The products' expansion potential is limited.
- Channels of distribution are kept by the competitors, and as a new brand, we have to fight for a place in the distribution channel.
- We do not have product image and reputation. But we do not have negative image either.
- So, we will postpone consumer communication activities for a while.
- Because of start-up costs, we will not be able to have a flexible pricing policy.
- Unfortunately, we do not have enough data to analyze the market.
- Location of the production will be in China/Taiwan, so it may cause a time delay in the distribution of the goods.
- We cannot use the benefits of economies of scale.
- Experience of the personnel will not be enough to compete in the market.

9.3 Competitive Advantages and Success Factors

The writing instruments brand offers a lot of different products that have different features and different benefits to the consumers. By the help of our niche focused marketing, we can easily become recognized by the consumers.

Most of the competitors do not have professionals who have a strong background and industry experience. Having such a manager in our management team will help us to manage the entrance difficulties. Most of the competitors are manufacturers, and they allocate their resources to manage the marketing tasks and production tasks. As a new company, we believe in the power of focusing on the marketing side of the business. Outsourcing the production will make us flexible in the market.

Our entrepreneurial management style will help us to adopt the situations easily, which is not possible for other companies in the market. Furthermore, wider hierarchical structure keeps us proactive. The products' expansion potential is limited compared to other brands.

The competitors have very high brand recognition, but their product images are not clear in the eyes of the consumers. Brand loyalty is very critical factor for the products that have very low involvement of consumers. The brand loyalty of the consumers to our competitors is very high.

The competitors in the market do not prefer to have heavy advertisement campaigns, and they do not have clear marketing objectives. If we do not focus on the consumer communication campaigns, we will not lose anything. Most of the competitors import the goods from Asia, so delay will not be a big problem. Since most of the players in the writing instruments industry are nonbranded, we position ourselves as branded company.

Competitive advantages

The structure of the company is very convenient for implementing new technologies, innovative ideas, and quicker decision making because of its size and management.

Success factors

- Innovative response to customer needs
- Consumer loyalty
- Identification of customer needs

- Aggressive commitment when required
- Cooperative trade relations
- High product quality
- Patent protection
- Ability to deliver high value to user
- Managerial ability and experience
- Quick decision and action capability

Key vulnerabilities

- Channels of distribution are kept by the competitors.
- Do not have a product image and reputation.
- Because of start-up costs, we will not be able to have a flexible pricing policy.
- There is no brand loyalty.
- Cannot use the benefits of economies of scale.
- Experience of the personnel will not be enough to compete in the market.

9.4 Scenarios and Opportunities

9.4.1 *Positive and Negative Scenarios for Industry*

Negative scenarios

- Acceptability of technology in developing countries is not that high. Technological products can be used by a broad segment after a long period of time.
- The existing competitors can use their strengths in distribution channels to block newcomers.
- The existing competitors can develop similar fast writing, smudge-free, note taking products.

Positive scenarios

- Economic growth, political stability, and population growth rate create new consumers for the writing instruments industry.
- The existing competitors cannot react effectively and in time because of their hierarchical structures and large sizes. Also, they are production-oriented and establish their strategies on the benefits of economies of scale.

9.4.2 Business Opportunity

The opportunity in the market is fulfilling the need for effective note taking (quick, smudge-free, dense line, reliable) by a brand that has a simple and distinctive image and targets distinctive consumers and reaches them through specialized resellers. Also, existing competitors are not convenient for distinctive consumers, as they offer a wide range of products almost for anybody in the market. Furthermore, their size and structure do not allow them to act proactively and in time.

9.5 Strategic Objectives, Main Goals, and Main Strategies

9.5.1 Strategic Objective

To be recognized as a reliable and quick note taking writing instruments innovator.

9.5.2 Main Goals

Financial and marketing goals

- Communication objective is having a clear brand image by offering a product that has a distinctive feature to fulfill the need of quick note taking for a narrow target of consumers through specialized and selected resellers.
- Creating a unique and new roller ball ink category, *Speedy Ink*. Convincing customers that this is a new roller ball ink, which is completely different than other products.
- Financial objective is to reach a break-even point at the end of year one and to 30% profitability at the end of year three.

Operational goal
Optimizing the procedures and operations with the third-party business partner that is responsible for the production.

9.5.3 Main Strategies

As we define our target market as the existing one that is asking new products, then our growth will be based on Product Development, as shown in Figure 9.3.

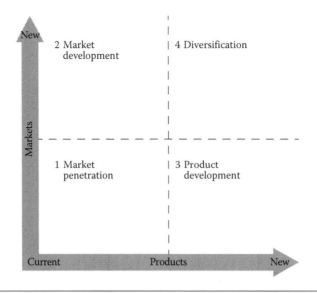

Figure 9.3 Components of strategy.

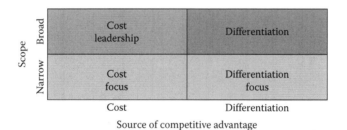

Figure 9.4 Generic competitive strategies.

According to the Porter's Generic Strategies matrix, we will also have Differentiation Focus, as shown in Figure 9.4, as we will narrow the target segment (writing instruments for quick note taking) and our competitive advantage will be based on the differentiation of our products by smooth writing, fast drying ink, and crispy lines.

Where an organization can afford neither cost leadership nor a wide scope differentiation strategy, a niche strategy could be more suitable. Here, our organization focuses its resources on a narrow and defined segment of a market.

Our business aims to differentiate itself within a small number of target markets (Turkey—students and business professionals). Within this defined target market, there are opportunities available for us to provide products that are clearly different than competitors' (they may be targeting a broader group of customers).

The primary consumer target includes middle- to upper-level business professionals and office workers who need reliable writing instruments to feel comfortable and to be sure that the writing will not discolor from exposure to light and possess superior color brightness for a long time. The secondary target includes government officers who need a documentary writing quality to be sure that the writings or signatures endure on documents for a long time. Moreover, others include doctors, journalists, and students need to write for a long time without ceasing and need to have clear writing without smudges.

10
Unified Tracking Solutions*

Mission

To be the leader in the arena, Unified Tracking Solutions (UTS) provides reliable and high-tech solutions with distinguished and valuable technological know-how in tracking systems in order to satisfy the safety needs of people who need traceability. While achieving this mission, UTS always considers quality, reliability, and privacy.

10.1 Environmental Analysis

10.1.1 Macroeconomic Analysis

10.1.1.1 Demographic   Population increase rate: Considering the average annual population growth rate in the period of 1990–2004, Turkey took place in front of India with the rate of 1.7%. The projections for the period of 2004–2020 show that Turkey's population growth rate will be 1.2%, and both Turkey and Ireland will be two countries in Europe whose population will be the fastest growing among European countries. Population will decline or remain constant in most countries in Europe. The low rates of growth trends in countries like the Netherlands, France, Sweden, and the United Kingdom are consequences of migrations.

In 2004, Turkey, with a rate of 1.52%, is the third country in Europe after Spain (1.64%) and Ireland (1.63%) whose population is rapidly growing.

Today, some of Europe's most fundamental issues include rapidly falling birth rates and the elder population. In this portrait, the

---

* This case study was contributed by Celal Ergüney, Fatih Okumuş, and Bülent Kama.

European governments are planning to reform their social security systems to make people stay longer in the labor market.

In this context, Turkey will be having significant advantages over the European Union with a well-balanced demographic structure and by increasing education and job opportunities.

Age distribution: The target age group is between 15 and 54 years. According to the regional distribution and educational status of this age group, the target audiences can be filtered again. In Turkey, more than 38 million people are between 15 and 54 years. Table 10.1 shows the age distribution in Turkey.

Educational level: Among 38 million of the population aged 18–54, more than 15 million has a higher education.

10.1.1.2 Judicial–Political Going through one-party power shows that stability would continue. Political crises in the Middle East region of Turkey constitute a risk of chaos. Restructuring of the Arab region toward democracy slowly turns toward capitalism. This is an opportunity for Turkish goods in the region.

Table 10.1 Age Distribution in Turkey

AGE GROUP	TOTAL	MALE	FEMALE
0–4	5,793,906	2,978,972	2,814,934
5–9	6,436,827	3,303,329	3,133,498
10–14	6,411,658	3,288,472	3,123,186
15–19	6,157,033	3,159,723	2,997,310
20–24	6,240,573	3,181,804	3,058,769
25–29	6,512,838	3,295,102	3,217,736
30–34	5,727,699	2,885,151	2,842,548
35–39	5,072,441	2,565,112	2,507,329
40–44	4,725,800	2,379,314	2,346,486
45–49	4,085,065	2,057,626	2,027,439
50–54	3,565,669	1,781,029	1,784,640
55–59	2,788,858	1,369,618	1,419,240
60–64	2,067,714	981,178	1,086,536
65–69	1,698,583	781,165	917,418
70–74	1,373,077	629,241	743,836
75–79	1,069,961	441,289	628,672
80–84	578,879	212,383	366,496
85–89	182,188	58,552	123,636
90+	97,487	27,473	70,014

Table 10.2   Income Distribution in Turkey

GROUPS OF 20%	TURKEY		URBAN		RURAL	
	2004	2005	2004	2005	2004	2005
Total	100.0	100.0	100.0	100.0	100.0	100.0
First 20%	6.0	6.1	6.4	6.4	6.3	6.1
Second 20%	10.7	11.1	10.8	11.5	11.2	11.3
Third 20%	15.2	15.8	15.2	16.0	15.8	15.9
Fourth 20%	21.9	22.6	21.4	22.6	22.7	22.6
The fifth of 20	46.2	44.4	46.1	43.5	43.9	44.2
Gini coefficient	0.40	0.38	0.39	0.37	0.37	0.38
	TURKEY		URBAN		RURAL	
	2004	2005	2004	2005	2004	2005
TYPES OF INCOME	%	%	%	%	%	%
Total	100.0	100.0	100.0	100.0	100.0	100.0
Salary and wages	38.7	39.2	44.5	45.6	23.9	23.4
Wages	3.5	3.3	2.9	2.8	5.0	4.7
Entrepreneur	31.8	28.8	25.7	22.2	47.5	44.8
Real estate	2.7	2.9	3.2	3.6	1.3	1.2
Securities	2.2	2.7	2.3	2.9	2.0	2.2
Transfer	21.2	23.0	21.6	22.8	20.2	23.6

10.1.1.3 Economic   Income distribution: Proportional distribution of annual income by income groups, 2004 and 2005. The share of wages and salary income are more than other income types. Annual disposable income of 39.2% is wage and salary income, and 28.8% is entrepreneurs income'. Table 10.2 shows the income distribution in Turkey.

Inflation: Inflation rate in June 2011 was 6.24.

Unemployment rate: Unemployment rate in Turkey decreased to 9.9% in June, which was about 14% in recent years.

Exchange rate policy: A policy of floating exchange rate continues, which forces the industry to manage this risk. Imports will also affect the industry.

10.1.2 Competition Analysis

Companies in the industry are mostly focused on vehicle tracking systems. No company has a total solution covering the whole market (end users, corporate customers, bicycles, etc.). Only Arvento, which is the most powerful competitor in the market, offers some integrated services, but they are also not focused on the mobile user market. There is no special product or service designed for end users in the market.

10.1.2.1 Rivalry Arvento: Arvento was established in Turkey in order to produce mobile technologies. It produces packaged software and hardware. As of today, its products are exported to 18 countries. The company is the market leader, which serves more than 9,000 customers and 120,000 vehicles. Other than the standard vehicle tracking solutions, the rest are as follows:

- Temperature control and monitoring systems
- Ready mix concrete dispatch and fleet management system
- Public transport and urban mass transit administration tools
- Emergency operations management system
- Staff transport vehicles monitoring and control system
- Fleet maintenance and service tracking system
- Safe ride control system
- Taxi/towing management system

Mobiliz: Mobiliz Information and Communication Technologies is an R&D company founded in 2004 to produce integrated systems that are parallel to the most recent technological developments. It produces and sells vehicle tracking systems. As of 2011, it has a staff of 45 people and more than 6000 customer portfolio. Its activities continue in Cyberpark Bilkent, Ankara Technology Development Zone.

Elcobil: Elcobil was founded in 2004 to produce innovative vehicle tracking systems. This company is analyzed because they supply several integrated solutions for different industries by using tracking systems. Other than the standard vehicle tracking solutions, the rest are as follows:

- Ambulance tracking and task management
- Vehicle allocation and task management
- GIS desktop software
- Ready-mixed concrete planning and control
- Armored vehicle and money tracking system

- Tour reporting
- Road risk assessment and control system
- Temperature and humidity monitoring system
- Taxi security system
- Alarm monitoring center
- Staff transport vehicles monitoring and control system
- Route planning and control

10.1.2.2 Suppliers   Since there are many firms in the sector that offer motor vehicle tracking systems, products, and services, it reduces the sellers' power in the field. However, the companies that will offer products and services for pedestrian or pedal user group will keep the power in their hands.

10.1.2.3 Customers   Since there are several companies supplying services and products in the vehicle tracking market, customers can use their power against suppliers. But for other products and services like end-user systems, customers do not have the same power because of poor competition in the market. Furthermore, even these systems bring cost efficiency for the companies that use tracking systems, which is not crucial for their core business. They can discontinue using these systems any time they want.

10.1.2.4 Substitutes   Although there are no products that can be directly called as substitutes, computer manufacturers, navigation companies, or smartphone manufacturers can get position in the market at any moment. Due to the small market size, these companies probably do not enter the industry at the moment, but they must be taken into consideration seriously.

10.1.2.5 New Arrivals   Since existing companies have high shares and due to the need of strong know-how about the technology, it is extremely difficult for new firms to enter the industry. Furthermore, competitors like Arvento and Mobiliz are located in the market for many years, and they have strong customer loyalties.

High investment is required to enter the market. During the development phase of integrated products and services, companies

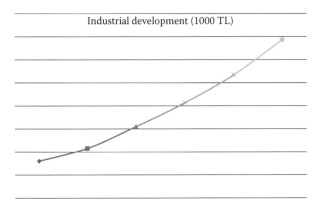

Industrial development (1000 TL)

Figure 10.1   Industrial development.

must hire qualified and experienced employees. Plus, a widespread service network throughout the country should be established. In addition, costs to create integrated solutions are higher than the existing players'.

10.1.3 Industry Life Cycle

Industry is at growth stage, and it is open to competition. By differentiated products with reasonable prices, companies can obtain competitive advantages. Competitors in the industry are directed toward institutional solutions, and they overlook the end-user market. Industrial development is shown in Figure 10.1.

10.2 Internal Analysis

We are going to provide GPS+GPRS integrated tracking system solutions for the retail market. Products will be designed in Turkey by our R&D group and will be manufactured in the People's Republic of China. This design and manufacturing function will be the responsibility of our R&D team.

In order to position our products in the retail market, existing distributers will be used to reach the sales channels and market. To position our product in the market and to manage our brand, we will build up a marketing team.

In order to serve technical infrastructure for our postsales services, we will build a powerful data center that will be managed by our technology team. There will be a team managing the postsales services channels. We will have partners that will be dealing with the end users. We will sell the necessary IT infrastructure services to our partners as a wholesaler.

There will be different channel structures for the postsales services functions. There will be partner firms that will operate the tracking system, provide the customer service supports, and perform the billing and charging operations. Partners will charge the end users on a monthly subscription basis.

10.2.1 Human

The company will be providing high-tech key turn solutions to its customers and has plans to achieve this goal by hiring talented people with a strong technological background. The organizational structure of the company is shown earlier.

10.2.2 Financial

The company has sufficient financial power to operate in this area. Since all the products or solutions include R&D and high technology and software development, Tubitak Teydep project support is acquired for financing the R&D activities of the company.

10.2.3 Physical

The main office and R&D laboratory of the company is located in Tubitak Techno-Park, Gebze, in order to take the benefits of the tax reduction and low rental costs.

10.2.4 Technological

The company will be providing high-tech key turn solutions to its customers. The company is capable of providing high-tech solutions in tracking systems by making integrations, combining existing products and developing software to form a new product or solution. Solutions are mainly based on GPS (global positioning system) to determine global coordinates of the objects, and GPRS (general packet radio services) and RF (radio frequency) to transmit the position of an object. Solutions also include supplying extra power to the system, which is very important in landscapes. Different GPS modules, transmitters, and power supplies are used depending on the requirements of the targeted market.

10.2.5 Business Strengths and Weaknesses

Strengths   The company's organizational strength comes from its ability to generate new high-tech solutions by using existing products and making new developments by a limited but highly motivated and qualified people. This strength is also supported by tax-free R&D activities for technological projects. Another strength is the customer satisfaction realized via customer-oriented postsales channel structure.

Weaknesses   The company's main weakness is a lack of reputation.

10.3 Competitive Advantages

The company has a distinguished and valuable technological know-how in this field, which is very difficult to imitate. Although it is possible to reach GPS and GPRS modules or products, it is difficult to form a new product integrating those products and making necessary developments. This approach requires very detailed knowledge of the technology and understanding of the internals of products. Additionally, the company has a strong sales channel structure, creative marketing capabilities, and customer-oriented postsales services.

10.4 Scenarios and Opportunities

10.4.1 Positive and Negative Scenarios for Industry

Positive scenarios

- The growing economy of Turkey will also have positive impacts on logistics, transportation, and tourism sectors, which will bring more demand to the tracking products.

- Increase in per capita income and changing trends toward nature will increase the interests for outdoor activities.

Negative scenarios

- The crisis in Europe triggers the global economic crisis. This may cause an economic failure in Turkey as well, which may shrink the end-user market.
- Global players can turn into our industry and build solutions by which creating serious competition.
- In case of any failures in GPS technologies, products will be useless.

10.4.2 Business Opportunity

By producing high-tech and value-added unique solutions to end users, we will fill the gap in the tracking market. Easy-to-reach products and map integrated with visual tracking and reporting tools will be our weapons.

10.5 Main Goals and Main Strategies

10.5.1 Main Goals

Financial and marketing goals

- Our main marketing objective is to deploy easy-to-reach innovative tracking solutions for end users.
- Our financial objective is to get financial support from the government for R&D projects.

Operational goals

Our goal is to set a perfect communication structure for the customer and partner.

10.5.2 Main Strategy

Our corporate strategy is to penetrate national- and regional-wide areas by concentric diversification from retail tracking to enterprise markets, and by using differentiation as a competitive advantage, which is shown in Figure 10.2.

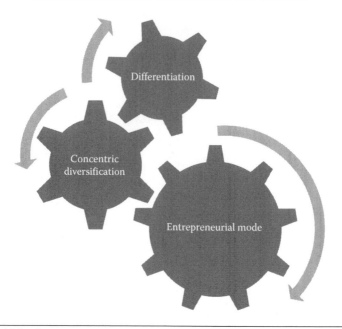

Figure 10.2   Corporate strategy.

11

ABLER BY ROBOMEDIKA*

We will create an innovative brand and establish a company that designs and produces innovative medical machinery. The company will touch patients' lives and make life easier for handicapped people. The brand is Abler, which will be the innovative and new generation wheelchair and will be designed by Robomedika engineers.

Vision

Being the best in everything we do. Serving people with an excellent care and high quality.

Mission

Carrying health assistance to a better position and making life easier for patients.

11.1 Environmental Analysis

11.1.1 Macroeconomic Analysis

See Table 11.1.

11.1.2 Competition Analysis

Based on the competition analysis shown in Table 11.2, statuses of competitive forces are obtained, and they are shown in Figures 11.1 and 11.2.

11.2 Internal Analysis

Tables 11.3 and 11.4 show the business history and accordingly the strengths and weaknesses of the firm based on a functional approach.

---

* This case study was contributed by Sinem Yılmaz Aslan and Ahmet Köklü.

155

Table 11.1 Macroeconomic Analysis Form

Category	Factor	Customers	Government	Financial Institutions	Suppliers	Shareholders	Employees
DEMOGRAPH	Population Growth					1	1
	Age Pattern					3	2
	Emigration Trends of the Population					2	2
	Birth and Death Ratios					2	2
	Education Level					1	1
ECONOMIC	Change in GDP					1	1
	Income Distribution					1	1
	Interest Rates					2	2
	Volume of Cash in the Market					1	1
	Inflation Rate					2	2
	Unemployment Rate					3	3
	Foreign Exchange Policy					1	1
	Saving and Consuming Trends					3	3
LEGAL–POLITICAL	Tax Laws					3	3
	Laws against Monopolization					3	3
	Incentives					1	1
	Green Laws					2	2
	Business Law					2	2
	Political Stability					1	1
TECHNOLOGICAL	R&D Expenditures					1	1
	Innovation Opportunities					1	1
	New Products					3	3
	Acceleration of Technological Changes					3	3
	Fastness of the Product Supply Process					1	1
	Increase of Efficiency by Automation					1	1
SOCIOCULTURAL	Changes in Lifestyles					1	1
	Expectancy of the Population for Career					2	2
	Changes in the Family Structures					3	3
	Changes in Personal Values and Belief					2	2

1, change for the better; 2, same as before; 3, change for the worse.

Table 11.2 Competition Analysis Form

	High	Normal	Low
FIRMS IN THE INDUSTRY			
Quantity of Firms in the Industry			+
Growth Rate of the Industry		+	
Differences and the Specialties of the Products		+	
Fixed Costs	+		
Cost to Leave the Industry	+		
Costs of the Companies in the Industry Related with the Company Size	+		
THREATS OF NEW COMPANIES			
Firms Which Have the Customer-Firm Loyalty			+
The Equity Needed to Enter the Industry	+		
Ability to Reach Channel of Distribution			+
Cost Advantage Related with Experience	+		
Barriers to Enter the Industry	+		
CUSTOMERS			
The Share of the Customer in the Wholesale	+		
Potential of Production of the Products by Integration	+		
Alternative Suppliers			+
Cost of the Change of the Suppliers	+		
Flexibility in the Prices			+
The Importance of the Product for the Customers	+		
Quantity of Firms in the Industry and the Production Place			+
SUPPLIERS			
Unit Products Sale		+	
Substitute Goods in the Market			+
Potential of Production of the Products by Integration	+		
The Share of the Sale of the Supplier	+		

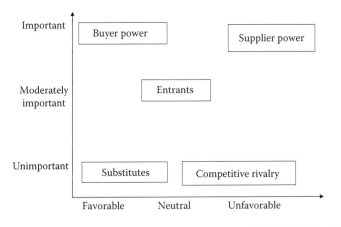

Figure 11.1   Competitive forces.

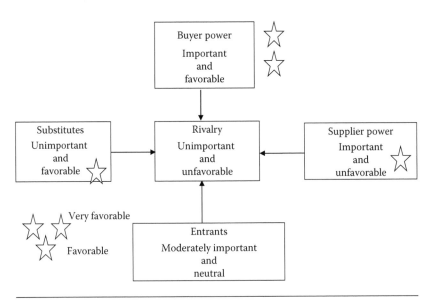

Figure 11.2   Competitive forces status.

11.3 Competitive Advantages and Success Factors

Ottobock is a German company dominating the sector as a world market leader. They not only have great financial power but also have an army of design engineers giving them the very best product designs and high-quality new products. Their key vulnerabilities seem to be their high costs and high profit appetites that lead them to high prices.

Medica 2000 is the biggest Turkish company in the medical sector. They are mainly focused on mass production of regular wheelchairs.

Table 11.3 Business History Summary Table

	MANPOWER	TECHNOLOGY	ORGANIZATION AND MANAGEMENT	OPERATIONAL FACTORS	PRODUCT AND MARKET POSITIONS	FINANCIAL FACTORS (X1000)
Year 2015	No. of employees: 40 15 clerks, 25 laborers	Increased production lines and capacity.	• CEO • Production and R&D dept. • Sales dept. • Dealer network • Governmental and key account sales • After-sales dept.	A flexible organization chart where depts. are quite interrelated. Dealer network and R&D dept. will be the main focuses of the company.	We expect to have brand awareness and start receiving orders from both end users and companies. In this phase, we will start attending local fairs and advertising in industrial magazines. The major jump for the sales will start by arranging a local dealer network where every single dealer will have an annual minimum purchase limit and a showroom requirement. This way end users will be able to test the product, and producer will guarantee a minimum sales number.	2.5% of the Turkish, Middle Eastern and Caucasian wheelchair markets in growing phase (estimated to be approx. 10,000 units annually).

(Continued)

Table 11.3 (*Continued*) Business History Summary Table

	MANPOWER	TECHNOLOGY	ORGANIZATION AND MANAGEMENT	OPERATIONAL FACTORS	PRODUCT AND MARKET POSITIONS	FINANCIAL FACTORS (X1000)
Year 2014	No. of employees: 10 5 clerks, 5 laborers	Less delivery date with more spare parts stock. Some demonstration units for major health facilities.	Labor will be separated from the clerks so that everyone can focus and expertise in their own responsibilities. We will hire one additional sales personnel who will be traveling around the country to be able to reach more end users.	Every partner will be responsible from their own dept. We will hire only for production dept. and end-user sales dept.	We will be delivering demo units to major hospitals and rehabilitation centers, face-to-face presentations and demonstrations to second circle of networks.	0.5% of the Turkish wheelchair market (approx. 500 units annually).
Year 2013	No. of employees: 9 4 clerks, 5 laborers	Order-based production (JIT). No stock machines.	We will hire one CNC operator who also knows welding. Four partners of the company will also assist production.	End-user sales B2B sales Government tenders Production and R&D each partner will be responsible from his dept. and will also support production.	Starting with personal contacts, friends, closest network that will be willing to pay for an untested product of a small producer.	0.05%—Size of Turkey wheelchair market is approx. 100,000 units per year, we aimed to sell 50 units in 2013 15,000 TL unit price 750,000 TL expected turnover.

Table 11.4 Functional Approach Worksheet

	FACTORS	STRENGTHS/ WEAKNESSES
Marketing	Firm's products/services; breadth of product line	S
	Concentration of sales in a few products or to a few customers	W
	Ability to gather needed information about markets	S
	Market share or submarket shares	S
	Product/service mix and expansion potential	S
	Channels of distribution: number, coverage, and control	S
	Effective sales organization	S
	Product/service image, reputation, and quality	W
	Imaginative, efficient, and effective sales promotion and advertising	W
	Pricing strategy and pricing flexibility	W
	Procedures for digesting market feedback and developing new products, services, or markets	W
	After-sale service and follow-up	W
	Goodwill/brand loyalty	W
Finance and accounting	Ability to raise short-term capital	W
	Ability to raise long-term capital: debt/equity	S
	Corporate-level resources	W
	Cost of capital relative to industry and competitors	W
	Tax considerations	S
	Relations with owners, investors, and stockholders	S
	Leverage positions	S
	Cost of entry and barriers to entry	W
	Price-to-earnings ratio	S
	Working capital; flexibility of capital structure	W
	Effective cost control, ability to reduce costs	S
	Financial size	W
	Efficient and effective accounting system for cost, budget, and profit planning	W
Production/ operations/ technical	Raw materials cost and availability	W
	Inventory control systems; inventory turnover	W
	Location of facilities; layout and utilization of facilities	S
	Economies of scale	S
	Technical efficiency of facilities and utilization of capacity	S
	Effective use of subcontracting	W

(Continued)

Table 11.4 (*Continued*)   Functional Approach Worksheet

	FACTORS	STRENGTHS/ WEAKNESSES
	Degree of vertical integration, value added, and profit margin	S
	Efficiency and cost/benefit of equipment	S
	Effective operation control procedures	S
	Cost and technological competencies relative to industry and competitors	S
	Research and development/technology/innovation	S
	Patents, trademarks, and similar legal protection	S
Personnel	Management personnel	S
	Employees' skill and morale	S
	Labor relations cost compared to industry and competition	S
	Efficient and effective personnel policies	W
	Effective use of incentives to motivate performance	S
	Ability to level peaks and valleys of employment	S
	Employee turnover and absenteeism	S
	Specialized skills	S
	Experience	W
Organization of general management	Organizational structure	W
	Firm's image and prestige	W
	Firm's record for achieving objectives	W
	Organization of communication system	S
	Overall organizational control system	S
	Organizational climate, culture	W
	Use of systematic procedures and techniques in decision making	W
	Top-management skill, capacities, and interest	S
	Strategic planning system	S
	Intraorganizational synergy	S

Their sales numbers are quite high, but the main reason of this success is their great financial power and the lack of competition in the Turkish market. Table 11.5 is a comparison of the firm with main competitors and industry average that ends up with competitive advantages and success factors of the firm, which are shown in Table 11.6.

Competitive advantages

- Functionality
- Risk appetite
- Low costs

Table 11.5 Comparison Table

	FACTORS	ROBOMEDIKA	OTTOBOCK	MEDICA2000	INDUSTRY
Marketing	Firm's products/services; breadth of product line	+	+	—	—
	Concentration of sales in a few products or to a few customers		+	—	—
	Ability to gather needed information about markets	+	+	+	+
	Market share or submarket shares	—	+	+	+
	Product/service mix and expansion potential	+	+	—	—
	Channels of distribution: number, coverage, and control	—	+	+	+
	Effective sales organization	—	—	+	—
	Product/service image, reputation, and quality	+	+	—	—
	Imaginative, efficient, and effective sales promotion and advertising	+	—	—	—
	Pricing strategy and pricing flexibility	+	—	+	+
	Procedures for digesting market feedback and developing new products, services, or markets	—	+	+	+
	After-sale service and follow-up	—	—	—	—
	Goodwill/brand loyalty	—	—	—	—
Finance and accounting	Ability to raise short-term capital	+	+	+	+
	Ability to raise long-term capital: debt/equity	—	+	+	+
	Corporate-level resources	+	+	+	+
	Cost of capital relative to industry and competitors	+	—	—	—
	Tax considerations	—	—	—	—
	Relations with owners, investors, and stockholders	+	—	+	—
	Leverage positions	+	—	—	—
	Cost of entry and barriers to entry	—	+	+	+

(Continued)

Table 11.5 (*Continued*)   Comparison Table

	FACTORS	ROBOMEDIKA	OTTOBOCK	MEDICA2000	INDUSTRY
	Price-to-earnings ratio	+	+	+	+
	Working capital; flexibility of capital structure	−	+	+	+
	Effective cost control, ability to reduce costs	+	−	−	−
	Financial size	−	+	+	+
	Efficient and effective accounting system for cost, budget, and profit planning	+	+	+	−
Production/ technical	Raw materials cost and availability	−	+	−	−
	Inventory control systems; inventory turnover	−	+	+	−
	Location of facilities; layout and utilization	+	−	+	−
	Economies of scale	−	+	+	+
	Technical efficiency of facilities and utilization of capacity	−	+	+	+
	Effective use of subcontracting	+	−	−	−
	Degree of vertical integration, value added and profit margin	+	−	−	−
	Efficiency and cost/benefit of equipment	+	+	−	−
	Effective operation control procedures	+	−	−	−
	Cost and technological competencies relative to industry and competitors	+	+	−	−
	Research and development/technology/innovation	+	−	−	−
	Patents, trademarks, and similar	+	+	−	−
Personnel	Management personnel	+	+	−	−
	Employees' skill and morale	+	+	−	−
	Labor relations cost compared to industry and competition	+	−	−	−
	Efficient and effective personnel policies	+	−	−	−

(Continued)

Table 11.5 (*Continued*) Comparison Table

	FACTORS	ROBOMEDIKA	OTTOBOCK	MEDICA2000	INDUSTRY
	Effective use of incentives to motivate performance	+	−	−	−
	Ability to level peaks and valleys of employment	−	+	+	+
	Employee turnover and absenteeism	+	+	+	+
	Specialized skills	+	+	−	−
	Experience	+	+	+	+
Organization of general management	Organizational structure	+	+	−	−
	Firm's image and prestige	−	+	+	+
	Firm's record for achieving objectives	−	+	+	+
	Organization of communication system	−	+	+	−
	Overall organizational control system	−	+	+	−
	Organizational climate, culture	−	+	−	−
	Use of systematic procedures and techniques	−	+	−	−
	Top-management skill, capacities, and interest	+	+	−	−
	Strategic planning system	+	+	−	−
	Intraorganizational synergy	+	+	−	−

Table 11.6 Competitive Advantages and Success Factors

	FACTORS	COMPETITIVE ADVANTAGES	KEY VULNERABILITY	SUCCESS FACTORS
Organization of general management	1. Flexible and horizontal relations facilitate decision making	✓		
	2. Participatory and sharing management	✓		
	3. Broad investment vision			✓
	4. Prestigious company name		✓	
	5. Experienced management staff undertaking responsibilities			✓
	6. Strategic planning and budget discipline			✓
Personnel	1. Competent, experienced, and responsible staff	✓		
	2. Qualified and young labor force	✓		
	3. Specialized staff	✓		
Production and technical	1. Ease of raw material supply		✓	
	2. Good supplier relations		✓	
	3. Registered trademarks			✓
	4. Effective use of subcontractors	✓		
	5. Cost advantage through extraction of sand from own sandpit	✓		
	6. Production control procedures		✓	
	7. Effective quality control		✓	
	8. Vertical integration	✓		
	9. Technical team competence			✓
	10. Product development capacity			✓
	11. Development potential of products	✓		
Marketing	1. Product diversity	✓		
	3. Pre-sales application service	✓		
	6. Technical support department			✓
	7. Strong references		✓	

(*Continued*)

Table 11.6 (Continued)   Competitive Advantages and Success Factors

	FACTORS	COMPETITIVE ADVANTAGES	KEY VULNERABILITY	SUCCESS FACTORS
Finance and accounting	1. Automation and integration through system investments, resulting in effective accounting, costing, and budgeting			✓
	2. Effective cost control			✓
	3. High credibility			✓
	4. Positive communication with shareholders, strong shareholder structure	✓		
	5. High equity profitability	✓		
	6. High working capital ratio		✓	
	7. High profit margin	✓		
	8. Long-term capital raising capacity	✓		
	9. Image of a tax-paying and strong company		✓	

Success factors
Price

Key vulnerability
Financial power

11.4 Scenarios and Opportunities

11.4.1 Assumptions

1. Turkish government increases the budget for social security and health-care system.
2. The economic growth of Turkey increases higher than expected.
3. Turkish government provides higher incentives for high-tech start-ups.
4. Caucasian and Middle Eastern markets for health support equipment will grow.
5. Euro/TL parity increases so high that Turkish companies have price advantages.

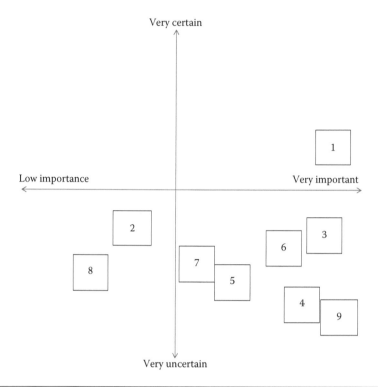

Figure 11.3 Certainty–importance grid.

Table 11.7 Developing Alternative Scenarios

		CLASSIFICATION		
	LIST OF UNCERTAIN EVENTS	IMPORTANCE	PROBABILITY OF OCCURRENCE	RATE
1	Increased budget for social security and health-care system	A	I	8
2	Higher economic growth	O	O	1
3	Higher incentives for high-tech start-ups	A	O	4
4	Growing Caucasian and Middle Eastern markets	A	U	0
5	Increased Euro/TL parity	O	O	1
6	Restrictions for low quality health-care equipment	E	O	3
7	Decreased transportation costs from China to Turkey	I	O	2
8	Russia gives importance to health-care equipment market	O	O	1
9	New developments in medical science	A	U	0

6. There will be strict restrictions for low-quality health-care equipment that may reduce Chinese competitive power.
7. Transportation costs from China to Turkey may decrease due to the higher return loads from Turkey to China.
8. Russia gives importance to health-care equipment market.
9. New developments in medical science allow handicapped patients get well.

By positioning the assumptions resulted from environmental analysis (shown in Figure 11.3), the following list of events are formed, and they are rated based on their importances and probability of occurrences. Accordingly, the list of events that have rates above 3 (shown in Table 11.7) are used for developing alternative scenario definitions.

11.4.2 Positive and Negative Scenarios for Industry

Positive scenarios

- Based on events 1 and 2, governments worldwide increase their budget for health-care and social security systems that increase the size of medical market. In addition to this progress, economic growth also improves the sales and profitability.
- Based on event 3, Turkish government gives high incentives to local start-ups in the medical field.
- Based on events 5 and 6, increased €/TL parity and the restrictions on low-quality Chinese products, Turkish brands may have best price/performance ratios that may help them in both local and global competition.

Negative scenarios

- Based on event 7, if Turkey starts exporting to China, transportation companies will be able to find return loads easier for their containers. This less likely case will decrease the transportation costs that may be a threat for Turkish medical companies.

• Based on event 8, new player means more competition. Russia currently is not active in the medical field; but if they give importance to this field, it may have a negative effect on especially Turkish companies.

11.4.3 Business Opportunity

High profitability and fewer players may point out the attractiveness of the medical market, but high R&D expenses and wide distribution channels require a great amount of capital for investment. So the market is quite attractive for financially powered big players but quite risky for start-ups.

On one side, there are high-tech global giants and on the other side, there are low-cost Chinese companies. It is not easy to compete with any side, and entry barrier to market is quite high.

As Turkey does not have a developed electronics industry, we need to purchase 70% of inputs from other countries, which makes us dependent on factors that we cannot control. Backward vertical integration is necessary, but it is not easy to realize.

The first positive scenario can be our Big Bang, in which market attractiveness is quite high and our product performances, costs, technical, and nontechnical competencies and management skills can help us take advantage (shown in Table 11.8) of this opportunity. Figure 11.4 shows the Big Bang as a business opportunity, based on the competitive advantages of the firm that can be used for catching the probable positive scenarios that may happen for the industry.

Table 11.8 Competitive Position

	WEAK	MEDIUM	STRONG
Brand, image, and reputation	+		
Simplicity of product/market focus		+	
Relative market (or niche) share	+		
Product and service performances			+
Distribution channels	+		
Cost			+
Responsiveness			+
Technical and nontechnical competencies			+
Financial strength	+		
Management skills			+

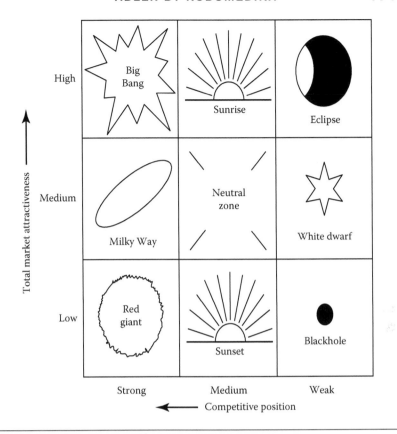

Figure 11.4 Business opportunities.

11.5 Strategic Objectives, Main Goals, and Main Strategies

11.5.1 Strategic Objective

Touch patients' lives.

We will focus on creating more value for our customers through innovative solutions and comfort. Our products should deliver better performance to our customers and provide superior health. Being innovative in the sector helps us to take place in the market. We should act as an entrepreneur by creating value and earning trust from the customers.

11.5.2 Main Goals

- 50 units in 2013
- 0.5% of the Turkish wheelchair market in initial phase (approx. 500 units annually)

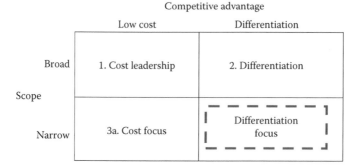

Figure 11.5 Generic competitive strategies.

11.5.3 Main Strategies

Figure 11.5 shows the differentiation focusing as a strategy. We will use unique technology, features, channels, and customer services. We will offer physical benefits to the customers with lots of unique features. Also, we will focus on a relatively narrow market segment and a buyer group.

We will bring special features and advantages to the product. Thus, for marketing innovative products, we should use marketing tools (e.g., by attending local fairs and advertising in industrial magazines). The major jump for the sales will be by organizing a local dealer network, in which every single dealer should have an annual minimum purchase limit and meet some basic showroom requirements.

12
Schneider Electric*

Schneider Electric SA is a Société Anonyme (joint-stock corporation) governed by the French Commercial Code with an issued capital of €1,962,394,928. Since May 3, 2006, it has had a two-tier management structure with a Supervisory Board and a Management Board.

From 1836 to today, Schneider Electric has transformed itself into a global specialist in energy management. Starting from its roots in the iron and steel industry, heavy machinery, and ship building, it moved into electricity and automation management. After 170 years of history, Schneider Electric has today become the solution provider that will help you make the most of your energy. Discover its transformation in the following:

- 1836: The Schneider brothers took over the Creusot foundries. Two years later, they created Schneider & Cie.
- 1891: Having become an armaments specialist, Schneider launched itself into the emerging electricity market.
- 1919: Installation of Schneider in Germany and Eastern Europe via the European Industrial and Financial Union (EIFU). In the following years, Schneider associated with Westinghouse, a major international electrical group. The group enlarged its activity to manufacturing electrical motors, electrical equipment for power stations, and electrical locomotives.
- *Post war*: Schneider gradually abandoned armaments and turned into construction, iron and steel works, and electricity. The company was completely reorganized in order to diversify and open itself into new markets.

---

* This case study was contributed by Gamze Karakaya, Dilay Savaş, and Evrim Karagöz.

- 1981–1997: Schneider Group continued focusing on the electrical industry by separating from its nonstrategic activities. This policy was given a concrete form through strategic acquisitions by Schneider Group: Telemecanique in 1988, Square D in 1991, and Merlin Gerin in 1992.
- 1999: Development of installation, systems, and control with the acquisition of Lexel (Europe's number two in electrical distribution). In May 1999, the group was renamed as Schneider Electric (emphasizing its expertise in the electrical field). The group engaged in a strategy of accelerated growth and competitiveness.
- 2000–2009: Period of organic growth and positioning itself into new market segments: UPS (uninterruptible power supply), movement control, and building automation and security through acquisitions of APC, Clipsal, TAC, Pelco, and Xantrex.
- 2010: Schneider Electric strengthened its lead in the development of Smart Grid, by acquiring the distribution activities of Areva T&D.
- 2011: Schneider Electric acquired leading software firm Telvent to reinforce its solution capability for the smart grid and mission-critical infrastructure.

Vision

Reducing reliance on foreign oil, carbon emissions, and energy costs of every project we install. A leader in high-efficiency *green* power solutions, including renewable energy.

Mission

Creating value by successfully harnessing the expertise of a highly skilled multidisciplinary engineering team in the design, delivery, and operations of high-quality sustainable energy solutions worldwide.

Basic Policies

- Business ethics comes first.
- The health and safety of employees is one of the most significant concerns.
- Managing a reliable business and service toward customers.
- Providing a successful technical knowledge and support beyond services.

- Conducting a proper annual maintenance of plants (turbines and panels).
- Respecting and protecting the environment with SE regulations.
- Aiming to reduce carbon footprints locally and globally.
- Managing an outstanding success in renewable and sustainable energy with an accurate rate of company growth.
- Becoming a signature in green energy.

12.1 Environmental Analysis

12.1.1 Macroeconomic Analysis

See Table 12.1.

12.1.2 Competition Analysis

Based on the competition analysis that is shown in Table 12.2, statuses of competitive forces are obtained and they are shown in Figures 12.1 and 12.2.

12.1.3 Industry Life Cycle

Figure 12.3 shows the industry at the maturity level.

12.2 Internal Analysis

Tables 12.3 and 12.4 show the business history table and accordingly the strengths and weaknesses of the firm based on a functional approach.

12.3 Competitive Advantages and Success Factors

Table 12.5 is a comparison of the firm with main competitor and industry average that ends up with competitive advantages and success factors of the firm, which are shown in Table 12.6.

12.4 Scenarios and Opportunities

By using the results of environmental analysis, the following list of events are formed, and they are rated based on their importance and probability of occurrences. Accordingly, the events that have rates above 12 (shown in Table 12.7) are used for developing alternative scenario definitions.

Table 12.1 Macroeconomic Analysis Form

	DEMOGRAPHIC						ECONOMIC								LEGAL–POLITICAL					TECHNOLOGICAL						SOCIO-CULTURAL			
	Population Growth	Age Pattern	Emigration Trends of the Population	Birth and Death Ratios	Education Level	Change in GDP	Income Distribution	Interest Rates	Volume of Cash in the Market	Inflation Rate	Unemployment Rate	Foreign Exchange Policy	Saving and Consuming Trends	Tax Laws	Laws against Monopolization	Incentives	Green Laws	Business Law	Political Stability	R&D Expenditures	Innovation Opportunities	New Products	Acceleration of Technological Changes	Fastness of the Product Supply Process	Increase of Efficiency by Automation	Changes in Lifestyles	Expectancy of the Population for Career	Changes in the Family Structures	Changes in Personal Values and Belief
Customers	1	2	1	1	1	1	3	1	3	3	3	1	3	1	1	1	1	1	1	1	1	1	1	3	1	1	1	3	3
Government	1	2	1	1	1	1	1	1	3	3	3	1	3	1	1	1	1	1	1	1	1	1	1	3	1	1	1	3	3
Financial Institutions	1	2	1	1	1	1	1	1	3	3	3	1	3	1	1	1	1	1	1	1	1	1	1	3	1	1	1	3	3
Suppliers	1	2	1	1	1	1	3	1	3	3	3	1	3	1	1	1	1	1	1	1	1	1	1	3	1	1	1	3	3
Shareholders	1	2	2	1	1	1	1	1	3	3	3	1	3	3	1	1	1	1	1	1	1	1	1	3	1	1	1	3	3
Employees	1	1	1	1	1	1	2	1	3	3	3	1	3	3	1	1	1	1	1	1	1	1	1	3	1	1	1	3	3

1, Change for the better; 2, Same as before; 3, Change for the worse.

Table 12.2 Competition Analysis Form

Category	Factor	High	Normal	Low
FIRMS IN THE INDUSTRY	Quantity of Firms in the Industry	X		
	Growth Rate of the Industry	X		
	Differences and the Specialties of the Products	X		
	Fixed Costs	X		
	Cost to Leave the Industry	X		
THREATS OF NEW COMPANIES	Costs of the Companies in the Industry Related with the Company Size		X	
	Firms Which Have the Customer-Firms Loyalty			X
	The Equity Needed to Enter the Industry	X		
	Ability to Reach Channel of Distribution		X	
	Cost Advantage Related with Experience			X
	Barriers to Enter the Industry	X		
COMPETITIVE POWER OF CUSTOMERS	The Share of the Customer in the Wholesale		X	
	Potential of Production of the Product by Integration		X	
	Alternative Suppliers	X		
	Cost of the Change of the Suppliers	X		
	Flexibility in the Prices			X
	The Importance of the Product for the Customers	X		
	Quantity of Firms in the Industry and the Production Place	X		
COMPETITIVE POWER OF SUPPLIERS	Unique Products Sale		X	
	Substitute Goods in the Market		X	
	Potential of Production of the Products by Integration		X	
	The Share of the Sale of the Supplier		X	

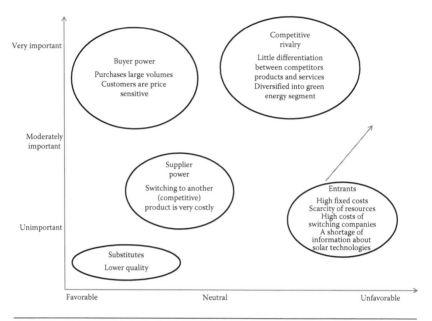

Figure 12.1   Competitive forces.

12.4.1 Positive and Negative Scenarios for Industry

Positive scenarios

- According to the Deputy of General Director, Ministry of Energy and Natural Resources, the share of renewable resources in electricity generation will be increased to at least 30% by 2023. This shows that government subsidiaries will be increased.
- As fossil fuel resources are expensive, demand for renewable resources will increase. Therefore, renewable energy ventures may also increase.

Negative scenarios

- It is hard to find proper places for both solar and wind energies in Turkey. Additionally, the investment cost of solar panels is quite high.
- As a result of economic instability, new investments may be low. Furthermore, energy and raw material costs would rise, capacity utilization would decline, and prices would surge.

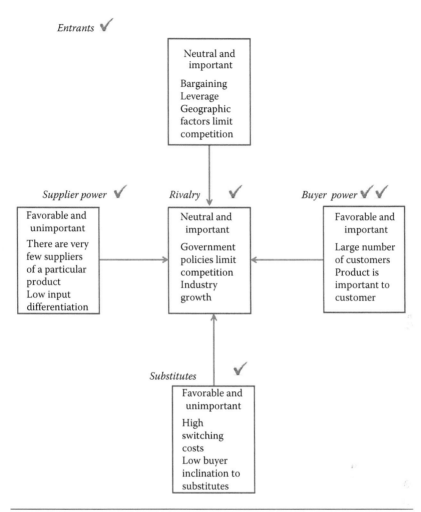

Figure 12.2   Competitive forces status.

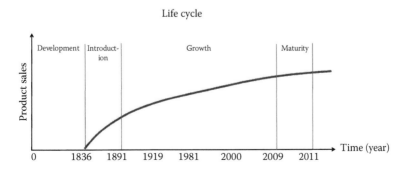

Figure 12.3   Industry life cycle.

Table 12.3 Business History Summary Table

YEAR	MANPOWER	TECHNOLOGY	ORGANIZATION AND MANAGEMENT	OPERATIONAL FACTORS	PRODUCTS AND MARKET POSITIONS	FINANCIAL FACTORS
2010	No. of employees: 123,482 61,911 production, 61,571 administration	Launched In-Diya LED based lighting system, partnering with Big C, solar energy project in Morocco, six universal electrical vehicles sustainable development projects, telemetry products with SCADAGroup	Strategic partnership with Masdar, EPC chosen, new smarter buildings with IBM, Vizelia, and DSX software management companies	Alstom and Schneider Electric will develop cooperation between the transmission and distribution business of Areva SE has more than 200 production sites and 140 distribution centers	Drawing on its global scope, the group has rebalanced and optimized its manufacturing and supply chain resources. The group launched a new stage in its industrial deployment in 2010. As part of the group's new organization, the power business production and supply chain resources have been globalized and combined under a single organization, with global operating responsibility. Previously, these resources were organized by region and reported to the various operating divisions.	Profitability € 1,720 million Capital € 2,175,672,728
2009	No. of employees: 116,065 55,125 production, 60,940 administration	Innovation and Technology Committee was set up in 2009 to promote the deployment of existing resources	Acquisition of Conzerv System, the recognized in the Indian energy efficiency market, inaugurated the Vinonsur-Verdon	Based on a Lean manufacturing approach, SPS is supported by the extension of Six Sigma and quality and value analysis programs	Around 7500 team members directly involved in R&D or technical engineering. Around 100 units divided among more than 70 sites in 25 countries.	Profitability € 852 million Capital € 2,102,016,200

(Continued)

Table 12.3 (Continued) Business History Summary Table

YEAR	MANPOWER	TECHNOLOGY	ORGANIZATION AND MANAGEMENT	OPERATIONAL FACTORS	PRODUCTS AND MARKETPOSITIONS	FINANCIAL FACTORS
		and consider the implementation of additional tools. The committee, which meets monthly, includes the division technical directors and members of the strategy and innovation department. The VELCRI electric vehicle with integrated fast charger project led by Renault is designed.	Salar Park in southeastern France, in partnership with Solaire Direct and Caisse des Dépôts Schneider Electric and Philips launched a new vision for interoperability in home automation and building control.	across the group. By deploying these optimization methods globally and sharing best practices, the group intends to life the operational performance of all its plants to the same high standard.		
2006	No. of employees: 119,115 52,115 production, 67,000 administration	Equipment and services for telecommunication, air, rail, road, and maritime trans-portation, water	2006 Award for Competitive Strategy Leadership from Frost & Sullivan, Merten in Germany,	Electrics and automobile manufacturing. The infrastructure market enjoyed strong growth in 2006. High crude prices are driving	To facilitate communication and enhance productivity, numerous Internet-based services have been developed	Profitability € 1400 million Capital € 1,789,154,928

(Continued)

Table 12.3 (*Continued*) Business History Summary Table

YEAR	MANPOWER	TECHNOLOGY	ORGANIZATION AND MANAGEMENT	OPERATIONAL FACTORS	PRODUCTS AND MARKETPOSITIONS	FINANCIAL FACTORS
		treatment, and natural gas and oil processing.	a leader in home automation that ranks fourth in its domestic market; OVA in Italy, domestic market leader in emergency lighting; AEM in Spain, a cable tray manufacturer, GET in the United Kingdom; and Clipsal Asia.	substantial investment in the oil and gas industry, notably in the Middle East, Russia, and North America.		
2005	No. of employees: 118,200 52,090 production, 66,110 administration	Terminal distribution, industrial and building automation	Growth flat forms • Building automation and security • Secured power • Sensors for repetitive • Machines • Installed base services	Manufacturing of track and recessed lighting for residential and commercial buildings	Acquired ABS EMEA, Invensys' building automation division in Europe and the Middle East. Acquired BEI Technologies INC, a manufacturer of customized sensor	Profitability € 1100 million Capital € 1,112,154,928

Table 12.4 Functional Approach Worksheet

	FACTORS	STRENGTHS/ WEAKNESSES
Marketing	Firm's products/services; breadth of product line	+
	Concentration of sales in a few products or to a few customers	−
	Ability to gather needed information about markets	+
	Market share or submarket shares	+
	Product/service mix and expansion potential	+
	Channels of distribution: number, coverage, and control	+
	Effective sales organization	+
	Product/service image, reputation, and quality	+
	Imaginative, efficient, and effective sales promotion and advertising	+
	Pricing strategy and pricing flexibility	−
	Procedures for digesting market feedback and developing new products, services, or markets	+
	After-sale service and follow-up	+
	Goodwill/brand loyalty	+
Finance and accounting	Ability to raise short-term capital	−
	Ability to raise long-term capital: debt/equity	+
	Corporate-level resources	+
	Cost of capital relative to industry and competitors	−
	Tax considerations	+
	Relations with owners, investors, and stockholders	+
	Leverage positions	+
	Cost of entry and barriers to entry	+
	Price-to-earnings ratio	+
	Working capital; flexibility of capital structure	+
	Effective cost control, ability to reduce costs	−
	Financial size	+
	Efficient and effective accounting system for cost, budget, and profit planning	+
Production/operation technical	Raw materials cost and availability	−
	Inventory control systems; inventory turnover	+
	Location of facilities; layout and utilization of facilities	−

(*Continued*)

Table 12.4 (*Continued*)   Functional Approach Worksheet

	FACTORS	STRENGTHS/ WEAKNESSES
	Economies of scale	+
	Technical efficiency of facilities and utilization of capacity	+
	Effective use of subcontracting	+
	Degree of vertical integration, value added, and profit margin	+
	Efficiency and cost/benefit of equipment	–
	Effective operation control procedures	–
	Cost and technological competencies	+
	relative to industry and competitors	
	Research and development/technology/innovation	+
	Patents, trademarks, and similar legal protection	+
Personnel	Management personnel	+
	Employees' skill and morale	+
	Labor relations cost compared to industry and competition	+
	Efficient and effective personnel policies	+
	Effective use of incentives to motivate performance	–
	Ability to level peaks and valleys of employment	+
	Employee turnover and absenteeism	+
	Specialized skills	+
	Experience	+
Organization of general management	Organizational structure	+
	Firm's image and prestige	+
	Firm's record for achieving objectives	+
	Organization of communication system	+
	Overall organizational control system	+
	Organizational climate, culture	+
	Use of systematic procedures and techniques in decision making	+
	Strategic planning system	+
	Intraorganizational synergy	+

12.4.2 *Business Opportunities*

Figure 12.4 shows the Big Bang and Milky Way as business opportunities, based on the competitive advantages of the firm that can be used for catching the probable positive scenarios that may happen for the industry.

Table 12.5 Comparison Table

	FACTORS	GREEN ENERGY	MAIN COMPETITOR	INDUSTRY
Marketing	Firm's products/services; breadth of product line	+	+	−
	Concentration of sales in a few products or to a few customers	−	−	−
	Ability to gather needed information about markets	+	+	−
	Market share or submarket shares	+	+	+
	Product/service mix and expansion potential	+	−	−
	Channels of distribution: number, coverage, and control	+	+	+
	Effective sales organization	−	+	−
	Product/service image, reputation, and quality	+	+	−
	Imaginative, efficient, and effective sales promotion and advertising	−	−	−
	Pricing strategy and pricing flexibility	−	−	+
	Procedures for digesting market feedback and developing new products, services, or markets	+	−	+
	After-sale service and follow-up	−	−	−
	Goodwill/brand loyalty	+	+	−
Finance and accounting	Ability to raise short-term capital	+	+	−
	Ability to raise long-term capital: debt/equity	+	+	+
	Corporate-level resources	+	+	−
	Cost of capital relative to industry and competitors	−	+	+
	Tax considerations	+	+	+
	Relations with owners, investors, and stockholders	+	+	+
	Leverage positions	+	+	+
	Cost of entry and barriers to entry	−	−	−
	Price-to-earnings ratio	−	−	+
	Working capital; flexibility of capital structure	−	−	+

(*Continued*)

Table 12.5 (*Continued*)   Comparison Table

	FACTORS	GREEN ENERGY	MAIN COMPETITOR	INDUSTRY
	Effective cost control, ability to reduce costs	+	+	−
	Financial size	+	+	−
	Efficient and effective accounting system for cost, budget, and profit planning	+	+	−
Production/ technical	Raw materials cost and availability	+	+	+
	Inventory control systems; inventory turnover	+	+	+
	Location of facilities; layout and utilization	−	+	+
	Economies of scale	+	+	−
	Technical efficiency of facilities and utilization of capacity	+	+	−
	Effective use of subcontracting	+	+	+
	Degree of vertical integration, value added, and profit margin	+	+	−
	Efficiency and cost/benefit of equipment	+	+	+
	Effective operation control procedures	+	−	+
	Cost and technological competencies relative to industry and competitors	+	+	−
	Research and development/ technology/innovation	+	−	−
	Patents, trademarks, and similar	+	−	−
Personnel	Management personnel	+	+	−
	Employees' skill and morale	+	+	−
	Labor relations cost compared to industry and competition	+	−	−
	Efficient and effective personnel policies	+	+	+
	Effective use of incentives to motivate performance	−	+	+
	Ability to level peaks and valleys of employment	+	+	+
	Employee turnover and absenteeism	+	+	+

(*Continued*)

Table 12.5 (*Continued*)   Comparison Table

	FACTORS	GREEN ENERGY	MAIN COMPETITOR	INDUSTRY
	Specialized skills	+	+	−
	Experience	+	+	−
Organization of	Organizational structure	+	+	−
general	Firm's image and prestige	+	+	−
management	Firm's record for achieving objectives	+	−	−
	Organization of communication system	−	−	−
	Overall organizational control system	+	+	+
	Organizational climate, culture	+	−	+
	Use of systematic procedures and techniques	+	+	+
	Top-management skill, capacities, and interest	+	+	−
	Strategic planning system	+	+	−
	Intraorganizational synergy	+	−	−

12.4.2.1 The Big Bang   Incentives other than feed-in tariffs for renewable energy investments:

- 99% exemption from annual license fees for the first 8 years of operation
- VAT exemption for domestic equipment for Investment Support Certificate holders
- VAT incentives for R&D activities
- Deduction of R&D expenditures from corporate tax base at a rate of 100%
- Income tax exemption (80% of salary income is eligible for R&D and support personnel), social security premium support for 5 years, and stamp tax exemption

The feed-in tariff for wind power plant is $0.073/kWh, and this amount can only reach to 0.11 cents with the addition of maximum local production premium. EPDK has granted 209 licenses with a total capacity of 7491 MW, in which 1725 MW of this capacity is in operation while 5765 MW is under construction.

Table 12.6   Competitive Advantages and Success Factors

	FACTORS	COMPETITIVE ADVANTAGES	SUCCESS FACTORS
Organization of general management	1. Flexible and horizontal relations facilitate decision making	☑	
	2. Participatory and sharing management	☑	
	3. Broad investment vision	☑	
	4. Prestigious company name	☑	
	5. Experienced management staff undertaking responsibilities		☑
	6. Strategic planning and budget discipline		☑
Personnel	1. Competent, experienced, and responsible staff	☑	
	2. Qualified and young labor force	☑	
	3. Specialized staff		☑
Production and technical	1. Ease of raw material supply, except for gypsum	☑	–
	2. Good supplier relations		☑
	3. Registered trademarks	☑	
	4. Effective use of subcontractors		☑
	5. Cost advantage through extraction of sand from own sandpit	–	–
	6. Production control procedures	☑	
	7. Effective quality control	☑	
	8. Vertical integration	☑	
	9. Technical team competence		☑
	10. Product development capacity	☑	
	11. Development potential of products	☑	

(Continued)

Table 12.6 (*Continued*)   Competitive Advantages and Success Factors

	FACTORS	COMPETITIVE ADVANTAGES	SUCCESS FACTORS
Marketing	1. Product diversity		☑
	2. Market leader in manufacturing of ready-made gypsum products	☑	
	3. Presales application service		☑
	4. Qualification and competence in ABS and ÇBS distribution channels	☑	
	5. Quality and branded products and ABS and ÇBS products	☑	
	6. Technical support department		☑
	7. Strong references	☑	
Finance and accounting	1. Automation and integration through system investments, resulting in effective accounting, costing, and budgeting	☑	
	2. Effective cost control		☑
	3. High credibility		☑
	4. Positive communication with shareholders, strong shareholder structure	☑	
	5. High equity profitability		☑
	6. High working capital ratio		☑
	7. High profit margin	☑	
	8. Long-term capital raising capacity		☑
	9. Image of a tax-paying and strong company	☑	

Fossil fuel resources are finite, and according to the International Energy Agency (IEA), the demand for oil has been increasing at a rate of 1.6% annually. The new policies seeking the reduction of greenhouse gas emissions along with the renewable energy targets and incentives, and the constant decrease in investment and operation costs of

Table 12.7   Developing Alternative Scenarios

LIST OF EVENTS	IMPORTANCE	PROBABILITY OF OCCURRENCE	RATE
In Turkey, the renewable energy sector and government policies have interacted and changed at a drastic speed over the last few years	A	A	16
Difficulty at the implementation of green energy facilities due to a high volume of entry barriers	A	A	16
Since the life of the fossil resources has been ending soon, demand of alternative resources will increase	A	E	12
To reduce our dependency on foreign countries, government subsidiaries will be increased	E	E	9
Since the investment cost of solar panel is quite high, people will relatively ignore its benefits	E	A	12
It is hard to find proper places for both solar and wind energies in Turkey	E	I	6
Solar and wind energies are preferable to generate electricity since they are environmental friendly	E	O	3
Importance of fossil fuels will decrease as they are scarce and expensive	A	A	16
Since green energy is essential for the survival of the planet, war games among countries could gain competitive advantages	A	E	12
Instability of national political affairs could jeopardize the industry power	A	I	8

renewable energy technologies promise that energy generation from renewable energy resources will grow significantly, which will reduce the demand for fossil fuels.

12.4.2.2 The Milky Way   Fossil resources will be ending soon, so that demand for alternative resources will increase:

- Today's global energy economy is faced with increasing energy demand, depleting resources, rising energy prices, limited availability and reinforcement of countermeasures to reduce pollution, and the effects of global warming.
- On the international basis, global firms are investing considerable amounts of their capital in alternative energy resources.

Large corporations are increasingly turning to renewable energy to power their operations. Companies are investing in renewable energy,

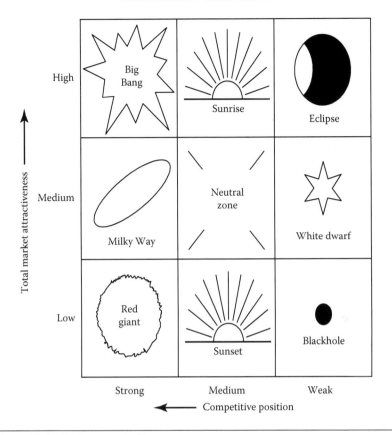

Figure 12.4 Business opportunities.

as renewable energy helps reduce long-term operating costs, diversifies energy supply, and hedges against market volatility in traditional fuel markets.

12.5 Strategic Objectives, Main Goals, and Main Strategies

12.5.1 Strategic Objective

Become a global leader in research and development in renewable energy and related technologies.

12.5.2 Main Goals

- Being one of the five companies in R&D in manufacturing solar panels and wind turbines in Turkey.
- Having two manufacturing plants in 2020. Expanding the production capacity to 10 MVA.

PRODUCT MARKET	PRESENT	NEW
Present	*Market penetration*	***Product development***
New	*Market development*	*Diversification*

Figure 12.5   Components of strategy.

- Offering the world's most advanced energy intelligence technology to customers at an affordable price.
- Building up strong financials and targeting a profitability of €1850 million.
- Reducing manufacturing expenses by 15%–20%.
- Transferring know-how and making money out of it, and minimizing the opportunity cost of owning a factory rather than leasing one.

12.5.3 Main Strategy

Figure 12.5 shows the product development as a strategy. By having the advantages of established channels, reputation, and brand name, high investment capability and customized products,

- Expand the market through high-quality solar and wind turbines
- Achieve the Schneider R&D mission:
  - Support, facilitate, and conduct research and development
  - Development capabilities across research institutions and organizations
  - Rapid product innovation
- Concentrate on cost reduction

References

Ansoff, H. I. 1970. *Corporate Strategy*. London, U.K.: Penguin.

Bütüner, H. 2015. *Systematic Strategic Planning: A Comprehensive Framework for Implementation, Control and Evaluation*. New York: CRC Press.

Harrison, J. S. and C. H. St. John. 2001. *Foundations in Strategic Management*. Evansville, IN: South-Western Publications.

Muther, R. 2011. *Planning by Design*. Kansas City, MO: Institute for High Performance Planners.

Pearce, J. and R. Robinson. 2011. *Strategic Management: Formulation, Implementation and Control*. Columbus, OH: McGraw-Hill Higher Education.

Porter, M. E. 1998. *Competitive Strategy: Techniques for Analyzing Industries and Competitors*. Florence, KY: The Free Press.

Rasiel, E. M. 1999. *The McKinsey Way*. Columbus, OH: McGraw-Hill Trade.

Vernon, R. 1979. The product cycle hypothesis in a new international environment. *Oxford Bulletin of Economics and Statistics* 41(4): 255–267.

Index

Printed and bound by CPI Group (UK) Ltd, Croydon, CR0 4YY

30/10/2024

01781020-0001